WRITERS
AGAINST RULERS

Writers
Against Rulers

Dušan Hamšik

Translated from the Czech by
D. Orpington

With an introduction by W. L. Webb

Random House New York

Publishers' note

This work is in no sense a report of the historic Congress of the
Czech Writers' Union which took place in Prague in June 1967,
but the author comments on it and describes its aftermath.
Indeed, he refers freely to various speeches and notably to those
of Ludvík Vaculík, Milan Kundera, and Laco Novomeský. The
publishers considered that it would add to the interest of readers
if these speeches were made available, and accordingly include
translations of them as an appendix. They were published in
Prague during the period of cultural freedom and have often
been referred to in the West but it is believed that this is the
first English translation to appear in print.

ISBN: 0-394-47022-2

Library of Congress Catalog Card Number: 70-143822

Manufactured in the United States of America

9   8   7   6   5   4   3   2

First American Edition

Contents

Introduction

Three weeks before the Soviet intervention in Czechoslovakia, on the eve of the meeting at Čierná nad Tisou, I stood with Pavel Kohout[1] in the doorway of the big children's store on Na Příkopě, the once fashionable shopping street that separates the Old Town of Prague from the hotels and office blocks of the New Town. In front of us some students were trying to control the crowd that pressed forward from the street, shuffling uncomfortably as those at the back leaned in to avoid the trams, but all staying to add their signature and their voice to Kohout's 'Petition of the Citizens'. (This *aide mémoire* from the nation to its leaders had been rushed out in a special issue of *Literární listy*[2] on the previous day to bind together the wobbling praesidium of the Czechoslovak Communist Party as it prepared to face the wrath of its opposite but hardly equal number from Moscow.) 'Speak on behalf of the people, which in these days has ceased to be an empty concept', Kohout had written. 'Act, explain, but in unity, and without concessions defend the road on which we have embarked and from which we will never depart alive.' Strong stuff, but a fair expression of the mood and will of that hot, excited crowd, and of others queuing up to sign at tables elsewhere in Prague and in towns all over Bohemia and Moravia.

Kohout, something of an actor as well as a playwright, was hopping about on tiptoe like a boxer, shaking hands with both fists, carrying on four conversations at once, exalted and fulfilled: a man who had risen to the occasion of a role he had been seeking in one way and another since he had gone into the streets in

February 1948 to cheer on the communist takeover of power in Czechoslovakia. More romantic than opportunist always, to him what had been happening in 1968 was indeed *obroda*, the rebirth of the revolution. Not all those in the crowd who were so anxious to echo his words now would have seen it just like that, but there was no doubt that this time was a high-water mark of the Czech people's unity and support for their brave new communist leadership.

It must have been rather like this, I suggested, in those great meetings in the Congress Hall in the early days of the Prague spring, when all the private questions were asked in public and suddenly there were answers that made sense. No, said Kohout, it wasn't like that—it was much better. 'Then, no one could really believe it was happening. Now everyone believes it can't really be stopped.'

Three weeks later, back in England, my strongest feeling when the first reports of the invasion came in, stronger even than anger, was disbelief. To turn the clock back to 1956, as the Russians seemed to be doing, negating the movement of the last twelve years of Europe's history and denying the real social and economic need out of which the Czech 'reformation' had grown, was an act outside the realm of reason. Like other people who had had the luck to spend part of that spring and summer in Prague, I had learned how necessary change had been, and, touched by the sense of possibility that was like extra oxygen in the air, I had come to see that sane and sensible revolution as a far more *likely* course for a socialist country in 1968 than the wooden absurdities of Novotný's modified stalinism. 'Mr Brezhnev's solution', I wrote on August 21, 'is not sensible, does not coincide with the realities of the situation.'

Since then, like the Czechs, though less painfully, we have all adjusted to the force, at least, of Mr Brezhnev's reality: the Kremlin's need was greater than Prague's, one might say, if one has the heart for irony—their clocks, after all, as Solzhenitsyn has reminded us, are slow in relation to our times. And as the last sad Dubček days gave way to the gloomy nonsense of the permanent purge over which Dr Husák uncomfortably presided, it became hard, once more, to believe that that spring had ever really blossomed; harder still, perhaps, to imagine how it seems now to those ardent students and housewives and shopgirls who felt and acted like citizens of a sovereign republic two years ago in Prague.

Yet for them and for all their people, to hold on to the reality of that time is the surest defence against the fate which the philosopher Karel Kosík outlined in an article in the post-occupation *Listy* in November 1968: degeneration 'from political nation into Czech-speaking or Slovak-speaking producers of steel and consumers of grain'. Politics, as he reminded them in that essay on 'Illusion and reality', is always 'a struggle in which one side tries to force the other to accept its view of reality and its interpretation of events'. In fact, 'Do not forget' was Dubček's message in the last speech he was allowed to make to the Central Committee, in September 1969. 'Do not forget,' he said, 'that in January we were prompted not by some individual subjective wish, but forced by the true state of the Party and society to set out on a new course in search of new and more effective ways of dealing with the problems of society.' It was indeed necessary to analyse what the Party had tried to do in 1968: necessary 'in order to defend its essential correctness, because one day, after we have solved the present negative tendencies in the Party and society, we will want to try and work out those principles again'.*

For us, meanwhile, for anyone who was moved by that decent attempt to develop a human and rational socialist society, it seems a minimal obligation to try to understand how it was made, and not to forget those who made it.

This account by Dušan Hamšík of the Fourth Writers' Congress held in Prague in June 1967 describes a crucial phase of that attempt. As he says in his postscript, many of those involved have seen that famous confrontation between the writers and the bureaucrats as a remarkably clear and coherent prefiguring of the larger struggle for freedom and democracy which was to involve the whole nation. But it was remarkable too for the way in which it drew together most of the streams of protest and criticism which were flowing so strongly underground in the latter days of Novotný's rule and would soon issue forth in a broad movement towards a politics that might correspond to the real needs of the

* The fullest translation of this important speech is in William Shawcross: *Dubček* (Weidenfeld & Nicolson, London, 1970)

people of Czechoslovakia. Then, as now, daily life for most thinking Czechs and Slovaks was an affront to the ordinary human sense of reality. All political systems are selective more or less in their use and interpretation of facts, but surely no other modern politicians have been quite so systematic in the suppressing or disallowing of inconvenient facts as those of the Soviet dependencies of Central and Eastern Europe. In Czechoslovakia, the country whose level of social and economic development corresponded least closely to that of the country for whose historical needs the strategies of Marxism-Leninism had been developed, this evasion of reality was most painfully evident, and who should register its absurdities more sensitively than the heirs of Josef Schweik? The point is made classically in an exchange in Václav Havel's[3] hilarious pantomime of the neuroses of post-Stalin bureaucracy, *The Memorandum*, which simply quotes a notorious remark of Novotný's about not being 'bullied by facts'. It was essentially the same point that economists like Radoslav Selucký and lawyers like Michael Lakatoš and philosophers like Kosík had been developing in the academic trade papers: the stalinist cult of the plan and the mindless worship of conspicuous production suppressed the facts about wasted resources and the stockpiling of irrelevant and unsaleable goods; the dogmatic interpretation of the 'leading role' of the Communist Party denied the fact that while class antagonism might have disappeared in Czechoslovakia, sectional differences as real and diverse as the variety of human interests had not and never would.

But it was the literary intellectuals, the writers and journalists, who were most gravely sickened by these constraints on reality. As Hamšík makes clear, the practical effects were extraordinary. Whole categories of normal literary and journalistic activity were simply eliminated. 'No documentary works, for example, were written; despite the wealth of material for such treatment during the past thirty years of our history, hardly a single eyewitness account of events, hardly a single volume of memoirs or descriptions of trials, political or criminal, appeared on the market. Apart from ephemeral essays reflecting the official prejudice of the day, virtually no books were published in which there was evidence of *thinking*, especially political thinking. It was the very literature of political commitment that was hit hardest by this state of affairs.'

What was happening, says Hamšík, was 'the suppression of the truly *engagé* by the bogus *engagé*'; and by the summer of 1967 the spiritual cramp which such a regime imposed on a humane and truly engaged socialist writer like Ludvík Vaculík[4] had become more intolerable than fear of the consequences of protest. Once again in Czech history it was time for the writers to 'deputise for other factors in our national life', as the congress's final resolution awkwardly puts it, by showing the way forward politically.

For frustrated radicals elsewhere, perhaps especially for the Westerner, it is part of the deep attraction of the Czech writers' struggle that at its most heroic moments it should be most plainly rooted in human reality. The Czech sensibility, unlike that of the Poles and sometimes the Hungarians, does not run readily to the grand gesture. Hamšík shows clearly how unnerved even many of his more progressive colleagues were when their broad-beamed, bull-headed Moravian brother got up and started to speak with such drastic candour. And yet one can hear quite plainly in Vaculík's brave speech the thumping pulse of an anxious human being. 'I spoke,' he says, in one of the exchanges with the *apparatchiks* Hendrych[5] and Bil'ak which followed, 'because I wanted for once to have things straightened out in myself. I challenged myself to say the plain truth about everything, because the plain truth is something I hardly ever find myself telling these days.' And when Hendrych, second in power only to Novotný himself, begins his blustering reply, full of crude misrepresentations of what had been said, Vaculík has to get up and shout back, unprecedentedly, 'That isn't true!' and again: 'That isn't either!' It is one of the most moving and characteristic things in the story, this absurd, vulnerable and magnificently human directness, butting through the brutal etiquette of the Party's power game. Indeed it was on just this note that Vaculík had ended his critique of Czechoslovakia's power system and his suggestions for a better one, his dreams of his country as a true socialist democracy: 'And if the men who exercise this power—just for the moment I shall break the spell that associates them with power and appeal to them as individuals with private thoughts and feelings—if they were to come here and ask us one question, can the dream be made true? then we should have to consider it a sign of good will and at the same time of supreme public spirit if each of us answered: "I do not know".'

It was as Pavel Kohout was reading out Solzhenitsyn's letter to the Fourth Soviet Writers' Congress that Hendrych had first walked out uttering his famous threat: 'You have lost everything, absolutely everything.' But perhaps not even Kohout's scandalous act was more abhorrent to the Party bosses than Vaculík's direct appeal to their humanity, throwing open a window in the closed system and dispersing, like a gust of fresh air, the mystification of dogma and cant with which communist bureaucracy covers a crude, essential opportunism.*

For a time, it looked as if Vaculík and the others had indeed lost everything; then, reinstated after January, as if they had been in the van of a cause that won a famous victory, with the official Action programme of the Czechoslovak Communist Party openly taking up all their criticisms and itself condemning 'contradictions between words and deeds, lack of frankness, a phrase-mongering bureaucracy, attempts to settle everything from a position of power'. And now they have lost again, every-thing Novotný's henchmen threatened they might lose. Vaculík, whose fate seems as vital a thread in the whole story of the reform movement as that of Dubček himself, added to the list of his crimes the 2,000-word petition (which may actually have tipped the scales in the Soviet decision to invade) and another open letter dangerously long after the invasion: he has been expelled from the Party once more and was reported at various

* Hamšík records how deeply Hendrych was embarrassed and disturbed by Vaculík's interruptions. The whole episode reminded me of Madame Furtseva's account at the Twenty-second Congress of the Soviet Communist Party of a meeting of the Party Praesidium held in 1957 to decide on the rehabilitation of the generals executed under Stalin. Even Stalin's closest henchmen, Molotov, Malenkov, Kaganovich and the others, concurred, she said—'And then, during the discussion, Nikita Sergeyevich asked them very quietly but directly: "When were you right, then? At the time when you voted on their fate with such a tragic result, or today when you claim to rehabilitate them? Answer me, on which occasion were you right?" This plain, straightforward question infuriated and embarrassed them.' (Quoted in Michel Tatu's *Power in the Kremlin*, Collins, London, 1969.)

times in 1970 to be awaiting trial, with Václav Havel and others, on what could have been made into capital charges.* The Czech Writers' Union has lost its famous weekly, its lucrative and admirable publishing house, all its funds and privileges—everything, except its offices in Národní třída and its virtue. That last item is a rare possession in Czechoslovakia in 1970, however. Václav Havel, it may be recalled, remarked in an interview some months after the Congress that it was disturbing that Vaculík, after getting such an ovation, actually gained only twenty-five votes when the selection for the union's central committee was made. But Marshal Grechko's tanks seemed to concentrate the writers' minds wonderfully. In June 1969, ten months after the invasion, when the pressures to conform were already considerable again, Vaculík was elected to the central committee with 242 votes out of 262, a vote second only to that given to the old poet Jaroslav Seifert who succeeded the exiled Eduard Goldstücker[6] as chairman. A year later the union is still refusing to recant, and astonishingly few Czech writers of any reputation have responded to the threats or bribes of the hyperactive Ministry of Culture. (Many of the Slovaks, however, led by Novomeský and Vladimír Mináč, are still treading a devious and difficult line of their own determined largely by personal loyalty to their compatriot Gustav Husák.)

In fact, few other sections of society in Czechoslovakia, hardly any other professional group of intellectuals, indeed, have been able to hold their ground so well. The universities and research institutes, the doctors, teachers and lawyers have been decimated twice over in the purge that has become a flux since the Plenum of September 1969, when Dubček began to slip down the steep slope which led to his expulsion from the Party, and perhaps his moral and psychological destruction, too, so anxious were the zealots to burn out his heresy. As for the Party generally, it seemed,

---

* By the end of the year, however, things looked a little less grim. The Slovak writer Vladimír Mináč, during a visit to London in November, indicated that the authorities were now anxious quietly to drop the charges; and subsequently the Czech Minister of Culture, Miloslav Bruzek, declared a qualified 'amnesty' for those who had signed the manifestoes of 1968. Perhaps the process of *gleichschaltung* has now reached the point at which the Czech leaders are ready to adopt the usual Soviet posture to writers and other intellectual independents—'Leave us alone and we'll leave you alone.'

at any rate for most of the time since the September Plenum, to be set on a course only too likely to end in the stagnation and disruption which Dubček prophesied. Perhaps Mr Brezhnev is bent on a practical demonstration of Stalin's adage about every right deviation being followed by an equal and opposite left deviation, though the terms of the proposition are meaningless to anyone but an old stalinist. But there were signs during the autumn of 1970 that even Moscow had realised that if the swing were to be allowed to go much further it might soon prove to be alarmingly counter-productive.

Meanwhile there is much to learn still from the whole Czech experiment and from this account of the writers' part in it. Hamšík reminds us how people survive in what Havel once called the pseudo-dialectical tension between stalinism and the Thaw; how the best of them managed to prise apart these cracked categories and reach toward a more rational synthesis. His book may convince us that, as *Literární listy* wrote in an underground number got out somehow on the day after the tanks arrived, 'the need which evoked these words will not come to an end, even if the sound of them is muted: the need which is expressed by the will to live in freedom, in human dignity, in an age of reason'. And it can remind us, as Vaculík said in his speech at the Congress, 'that power retreats when it sees and hears strong resistance ahead; not arguments—they will never convince the men in power, only failure, recurrent failure, with every attempt to do things the old way.'

One would like to believe, finally, that some Western readers of this book might feel scalded with shame at their complacent inadequacy to face the problems of our own 'softer' crisis—their barely audible complaints, for example, against the powerful *apparatchiks* of commercialism in journalism and publishing who are cheapening the very values of European humanism which the writers of Prague fought to assert. What can we do to help? people were asking feebly in London two summers ago. The answer to that question now, surely, must be that we can make it known to *all* enemies of those values that we have not forgotten Ludvík Vaculík and his comrades; and that, having learned from them, we hope to fight half as well on our front of the battle.

W. L. WEBB

I
Prelude to the crisis

Right from the beginning of 1967 it was obvious to anyone close
to the paper that this was a year when something was going to
happen to *Literární noviny*.[2] The pressures that had weighed upon
it for years past, far from abating, had grown heavier and more
ominous; there were forces at work now quite unconnected with
the country's intellectual life.

If nothing had been at stake but one newspaper the matter
would not have been so interesting. It would hardly have de-
served discussion. But in the particular situation of Czechoslovakia at that time *Literární noviny* offered a fascinating cross-
section and mirrored the total state of society. Clearly it was a
state of protracted crisis. It had already crystallised after the
Soviet Communist Party's 20th Congress—and several times
since then had been ripe for solution. Yet each time the solution
had been forcibly postponed, averted. It was paradoxical that in
our country, where throughout this century there has been a
strong socialist movement deriving from native traditions,
humanitarian and democratic, the bureaucratic-stalinist version
of socialism should have survived into the late 'sixties at all.
True, it was a Czechoslovak variant shorn of the most brutal
features of the original, but its essential nature was still there
and there was always a danger of reverting to type, lock, stock
and barrel. In 1967 Czechoslovakia's political system was a
belated, slightly reformed stalinism whose functioning conflicted
more and more acutely with the country's real needs, economic,
political, cultural and moral. A relatively advanced state, with

every prospect after the last war of successful all-round development, had become a stagnant one, marking time in the middle of a general slump.

Literární noviny was the only paper, apart from the Slovak *Kultúrny život*, that the powers-that-be had not managed to get under their control, officially or otherwise. A stream of critical thinking had been channelled into it which expressed things as they really were. Consequently it was a continual irritation to the men who wielded power and the target both of open campaigns and of invisible string-pulling and insidious regulations. For years it had been subject to persistent pressure designed to bring about a situation where the paper could be taken over from within, avoiding any frontal attack in public. The Communist Party leaders had, of course, the power to launch such an attack without question; but they also had enough sense to realise the risks that unconcealed use of their power would entail.

In the course of this *Nervenkrieg*, almost entirely concealed from the public, the Party's champions trained their opponents to such a level of skill that they made it virtually impossible for themselves to win the war by their usual techniques of intrigue and backstairs manipulation—techniques, it must be admitted, in which they had an expertise such as they sadly lacked in other fields. Their opponents were for the most part, of course, also communists, either in the central committee of the Writers' Union or on the editorial staff of *Literární noviny*. This is not as paradoxical as it might seem: it merely reflects the fact that what was going on in Czechoslovakia was a conflict inside the framework of socialism between the primitive restraints of stalinism on the one hand and the efforts to overcome those restraints on the other. It was a barren contest, from which little or nothing of creative, intellectual value resulted apart from a quantity of painful experience. But there was clearly no choice. The fight had to be taken on if we were to preserve that small measure of independence which remained to us—meaning by 'independence' anything short of complete subjection to the crude stalinist concept of socialism by which an ever diminishing group at the centre of the Party, and in the end a single individual, assumes all the powers and privileges including thought-control and an imaginary monopoly of the truth. Many a time we reflected bitterly that the task of standing up to these pressures was exhausting all our creative energy, and the need to resist manipulation was pushing wider human issues into the background, diverting our attention and our efforts into trivial daily tactics of a kind in which only stalinist executives could feel really at home.

It was a fight to establish points that ought to be self-evident, issues that need to be settled before the thinkers and creators can tackle the eternal and paramount problems of human existence, problems which any kind of socialism worthy of the name will want to pass judgement on. But so far it has not been able to, for it has had to waste time, energy and opportunities in this defensive battle against the retarding effects of stalinist distortion. We accepted the challenge because we had no choice. We consoled ourselves with the thought that if at least we bore honest witness in this wretched situation, it might help a later wave of progressive thought, writing and activity.

At the beginning of 1967, then, there was a disturbing intensification of pressure on *Literární noviny*, which had become the sole remaining forum of critical thought within the ambit of Czechoslovak socialism. The central bodies of the Communist Party used every device available to them under the existing system of authority which stemmed from the Party's 'leading role'. This meant that the editor-in-chief of the Writers' Union weekly was appointed by the Union's own central committee, but the appointment did not become effective until it was confirmed by the Presidium or Secretariat of the Communist Party's Central Committee. By a resolution of one of these Party bodies the post in question had been added to the Party Central Committee's 'cadre register'.[7] This meant that the central bodies of the Party were able not merely to approve, or withold approval of, the editor-in-chief but to influence his selection in the first place. In view of this the Writers' Union would not propose the appointment of a man who could obviously never 'make it'; the acceptability of a candidate to the Party *apparat* had to be taken into account as well as his professional qualifications. So an element of abnormality was therefore built into the selection process from the start, though this was by no means the only abnormality, nor the worst.

Milan Jungmann managed to do the work of editor-in-chief

for three years without ever being confirmed in his post by the Party. In this way the central bodies preserved an option to force Jungmann to retire at any time they chose without further ado. Throughout this period they were always seeking out and preparing alternative candidates whom they then kept in reserve in case their opponent should lower his guard for a moment. Some of the choices were quite ridiculous, men without the slightest qualification for the leading post on the paper or any adequate record of achievement in literature, journalism or even in cultural politics. But eventually a number of authors were procured who would certainly have been approved without difficulty by the Party's Central Committee and added to the cadre register. Equally certainly, however, they would never have won a ballot in the Union's own central committee, either because their literary works were too little known or because their character defects were all too well known.

During one of these periods when the Party's central bodies were viciously attacking Jungmann, refusing to confirm his post and demanding the nomination of an editor-in-chief acceptable to themselves, *Literární noviny* had to be run by a three-man presidium of the editorial board, a symbolic triumvirate of writers whom the Party could hardly veto (they were Březovský, Kundera and Otčenášek), while Jungmann's name only appeared as that of the man 'in charge of the editorial office'. In the same period the Party also intervened directly in the composition of the editorial board. The central bodies passed a special resolution requiring Party approval for individual editors and then refused to confirm the appointment of two of them. These two, A. J. Liehm[8] and Ludvík Vaculík,[4] were sent on obligatory 'creative leave'.

When the Writers' Union objected to these interferences and asserted its own responsibility for running its paper, it was told—through the Party members who constituted the absolute majority in the Union's own central committee—to put its own house in order and to make proposals for appropriate personnel changes. What sort of changes the Party centre meant had been made abundantly clear by all the previous vetoes and criticisms, which compensated for their lack of convincing argument by the severity of their tone. These statements had been by way of a softening-up barrage to convince the opponent that he must flee, or expect a direct and overwhelming onslaught. Further illumination now came from officials of the Party's Ideological Department, men who represented a certain liaison between the central bodies and the literary community and who, even in this tense period, tried to maintain some sort of *modus vivendi* and an impression of all-round helpfulness rather than succumb to utter cynicism. In private conversation these men would suggest that Number One, as he was called (or alternatively Comrade with a capital C, both being synonyms in the Party jargon of the day for First Secretary Antonín Novotný, the leading communist and perhaps the only one to deserve the title of comrade), was angry and impatient and would not put up with any more half-measures. Heads would anyway have to roll. 'So why don't we meet him half-way and sacrifice a few heads of our own choosing? We can make sure in this way that nothing too unpleasant happens to them. They can just leave the paper and do something else; no one will bother them and they won't lose by it. Otherwise . . .' At this point the Ideological Department officials would shake their heads as if they could already hear Number One's thunderbolts descending. As indeed they well might, for those thunderbolts always began by hitting the heads nearest to him, the heads of his immediate subordinates, all those reputedly reliable comrades in the *apparat* who were now found to have failed his trust and succumbed to various influences, and had to go.

There were long discussions in the editorial office and board of the paper, and in the steering bodies of the Writers' Union, as to the best way of reacting to these demands. Some advocated strict adherence to principle; rejecting retreat, or even tactical manœuvre, they would have stood their ground and called a spade a spade. This advice appealed to many. It was the fruit of years of painful experience of the excesses of 'cultural management'. Disillusion was not, of course, confined to the cultural sphere; it was now part and parcel of a wider recognition that the old model of socialism had failed all along the line—failed to secure economic welfare, failed to preserve democratic political rights and failed, above all, in the realm of human justice and moral and aesthetic values, things which under Novotný had been deformed and falsified. Arguably, then, it was both practicable and essential to stand one's ground. There were plenty of suitable issues. The very existence of censorship, concealed from the public and carried out (as we shall see) in constant violation of the relevant laws, modest as they were—this alone was a sufficient *casus belli*.

Others recommended a more cautious and flexible approach. It was pointless, they felt, to hit one's head against the wall of absolute authority in an empty gesture that would bring more loss than gain. Native opportunism apart, there was a solid core of sense in this argument, namely the time factor. Was it the right moment to revolt? The real reasons for our revolt would remain hidden: no one would hear about them. With its monopoly of the information media, supplemented by the censor's pencil, the ruling centre of the Party would have every opportunity to paint its own version of our rebellion and keep the public from any understanding of our motives. It would talk about the cliquishness of writers and the arrogance of intellectuals in general, intending thereby to stir up social resentment. Such resentment had in fact been exacerbated artificially by Party policies, but also enjoyed a certain tradition in Czech public life and still undeniably played a role.

This was the view that gained the upper hand. The immediate priority was to keep *Literární noviny* going, even if its scope would be much restricted. Retreat and manœuvring were inevitable if critical thinking about the state of society was to have a chance of making itself heard at all against the loud official counterblasts. Even the few candid opinions to survive in print, after all the string-pulling and in-fighting, were preferable to complete silence; they carried some weight in the creation of public attitudes which, if deprived of any critical outlet, would be even more misled and distorted than before.

So Liehm and Vaculík remained on 'creative leave' and Milan Jungmann decided to quit the editorial desk and make room for some arrangement that would, for a time at least, neutralise the Party centre's aggressive mood and allow *Literární noviny* to appear without betraying its purpose.

It was not until this stage that anyone on the editorial board thought of proposing me as Jungmann's successor. I had never remotely considered the possibility myself, having cherished ambitions of quite a different kind. Besides, after twenty years' work on newspapers and magazines I felt highly sceptical about the ability of journalists to educate public opinion under a system which fettered them with an increasing number of taboos. It was not only the explicit prohibitions; often it was just a matter of convention which many people had accepted and come to regard as a natural element of journalistic discipline. Czech journalism had never been especially militant or over-ambitious intellectually and over the years the poverty of journalistic standards had grown in parallel with the poverty of society at large. Even *Literární noviny*, though certainly the best paper we had, seemed to me too constrained. It lacked the freedom to ask questions which might upset preconceived notions lodged in people's minds over the years. I felt that even this paper had become inwardly warped, that the scope it offered was too narrow and its efforts rather futile.

I looked at Jungmann's working desk with its pair of telephones and piles of proof-sheets for the next number, heavily scored by the censor and then annotated with a maze of inserts and fresh corrections, all designed to rescue the unrescuable. Feeling useless and apprehensive, I refused the offer of his job this time. Little did I guess that in a few months I should be sitting at this desk after all, and that one of my first visitors would introduce himself by flashing a secret-police warrant.

But much was to happen before that. Milan Jungmann went on creative leave and was replaced by the senior official of the Writers' Union, its First Secretary Jiří Šotola. It was certainly the best solution for the paper at that moment; there could have been no more effective way of demonstrating that the Union stood behind its own journal. Though Šotola had been First Secretary for some time, he was foremost a poet, a sensitive, thoughtful and exceptionally good-natured man. What he most wanted was to be free to write again, so he was quite happy now to leave his more exposed position in the Union (where Juraj Špitzer succeeded him with the *ad hoc* mission of preparing the forthcoming Writers' Congress) and take on the editorship of *Literární noviny* as a purely temporary measure up to the time of the Congress. For Šotola it was a stepping-stone back to his own writing and it was agreed that someone else should take over the paper after the Congress —if there was still any paper left. For the clouds were gathering over *Literární noviny*, and to call them storm-clouds would be to put it mildly.

But again, much was to happen before the clouds burst. Notably, the Fourth Writers' Congress.

2

The Writers' Congress—up against the rulers

I must make it clear from the start that none of those who were later described as the chief organisers or 'stage managers' of the Congress had any notion that the event would have such importance ascribed to it, or that its repercussions would be so far-reaching.

True, there had been a good deal of uncertainty and anxious argument about the timing and preparation of the Congress, especially at the beginning of 1967. The field of cultural politics was strewn with chronic problems, some unsolved and some with no prospect of solution. They formed a conspicuous and explosive element in the more general distress of society, which was equally chronic and hard to treat not least because it was officially non-existent. So explosive, indeed, was this area that it alarmed both the ruling circles and the writers, though not in the same way. The date for the Congress was repeatedly put off and by the spring of 1967 it began to look as if it would not be held till the autumn or later. The Party leaders were clearly anxious lest the fiftieth jubilee of the October Revolution be marred by some critical note struck at the writers' meeting. They had had awkward enough experiences with previous Congresses, particularly the Second and Third. The official ideal would have been a Congress consisting of a few ceremonial harangues setting out the basic line (and previously vetted at Party headquarters to make sure there was nothing contentious or original in them); speeches from the floor in amplification and support of the same line; and a number of hackneyed resolutions to end up with. The writers' community no longer had any use for this kind of farce, nor indeed could enough actors have been found who were willing to play such roles with any conviction. It came as something of a surprise, then, when agreement was suddenly reached between the Writers' Union and the appropriate Central Committee Secretary in the Party, Jiří Hendrych,[5] for a Congress to be held in June. Part of the agreement was that the Congress would be a purely native affair with no visitors or delegations from abroad and that it would have a purely working, not ceremonial, character.

The phrase 'purely working character' was taken to mean different things by different people. Some assumed that it would deal only with literary problems on a technical plane far removed from everyday life; for others the words implied concern for the scope of literature as an active element in the state of society and in the creation of social awareness.

Hopes had been raised and then dashed time and time again by the vagaries of past policy, yet all the same the rather unexpected agreement on a date for the Congress seemed promising. Perhaps the Party's cultural policy would, after all, become more reasonable. Perhaps the leaders would at last take note of some of the well-founded complaints of the writers—including Party members. Perhaps some of the more scandalous kinds of discrimination and suppression would be dropped, or at least mitigated. Perhaps—and there were some optimists who believed even this —the Party centre was really interested in what our writers thought about developments in their own country and wanted to take note of their views in formulating future cultural policy—if nothing else.

Hopes like these came up in the discussion when the editorial board of *Literární noviny* met to consider once more my possible assumption of the chief-editorship. The board felt that a relaxation of tension might be on the way and that there would be a time in which attempts might be made to find common ground with the authorities or at least to establish fair ground rules. Expecting sympathy from the Party centre, they were willing in turn to offer a helpful response.

'Let's just concentrate for a while on doing a good, professional journalistic job,' said Ivan Klíma.[9]

Our paper had often been accused of irresponsibly 'tabling' new problems before the Party centre wanted them on the agenda, of destructively upsetting the well-calculated efforts of Party and government machines. So its publishers now hoped to encourage *détente* and assist the search for a tolerable cultural policy by refraining from articles of a sharply critical kind. They did not of course propose voluntarily to abandon the critical role, which is one of the duties of journalists as of all writers. But they were willing, for a time at least, to bypass those acute problems to whose public discussion the Party leaders of the day were especially allergic. What we had in mind was to come round to these touchy and painful problems of the present day by *apparently* ignoring them. We proposed to seek their roots in the past, either in authentic history or in that pseudo-history which preserves them in the national consciousness with the help of pious legends and special pleading.

How naive we all were! We imagined that we were making a reasonable compromise and simultaneously helping to throw light on the origins of the country's situation. When we finally mentioned this obliging plan of ours in official hearing it provoked an immediate and angry rejection; every article we proposed to publish was turned down with disgust; nothing seemed to the authorities such a direct threat to the Party's leading role as our idea of historical essays. But for the moment we were still convinced that this was one possible way to a solution of that national crisis which was reflected in our own field by suspicion and tension between rulers and writers, by an endless chain of conflicts and attempts to solve them by authoritarian measures.

I mention all this as evidence of the state of mind at that time of those 'Men of the Fourth Congress' who were later to be accused of organising it with malice aforethought, of systematically abusing it as a forum and of subtly stage-managing it through a group associated with our paper. I was then in closer contact with all the leading figures in the 'group', individually and collectively, than perhaps any other single person, and I cannot call to mind anything remotely resembling the hole-and-corner conspiratorial tactics now imputed to them. They were not the only people, of course, whose public activities made it harder for the Party centre to exercise its 'leading role'. They forced it to make concessions and their very demands suggested the outline of a different kind of socialism which exposed the weaknesses and falsehoods, both general and particular, of the stalinist model. But none of this could be called anti-socialist or anti-state activity, still less 'conspiracy'. Conspirators, after all, avoid publicity; even the men who denounced them were surely clear on that point.

Or should I perhaps assume that these people were deceiving me? Ivan Klíma, Alexander Kliment,[10] Ludvík Vaculík . . . Were these and other colleagues, with whom I had enjoyed years of friendship, sharing common interests, crossing critical swords and seeking solutions to our joint problems, really hiding their true intentions from me? This would only make sense if I had unwittingly deceived myself as well.

I well remember talking to other friends, too, after they had heard I was going to join *Literární noviny*. Some of them, who worked in the Party *apparat*, told me that even if the Writers' Union nominated me for the post of editor-in-chief I should not get Party approval. Their information proved quite correct. I learnt from these sources that my acceptance was regretted because the Party centre had a very radical plan in mind for *Literární noviny* which would involve a number of heads falling and blows landing on many shoulders, including perhaps mine. Another acquaintance in the same line of business had me in for a quiet talk and offered to tip me off a week in advance of the explosion so that I could leave the paper in good time. After taking his usual ration of cognac he started telling me that *Literární noviny* was plotting horrible things against the Party and the state; a few glasses later he was embracing me and assuring me he agreed with the paper anyway. What his real views were I cannot say, but he kept his promise to give me a tip-off.

There were more serious-minded officials on the ideological side of the *apparat* who shared, to a certain extent, our hopes of conciliation and did their best to bring it about. Even these people expressed their fears of the preponderance of 'hard-line' or 'dogmatic' forces inside the central bodies. If asked to guess how Number One and his immediate entourage would be talking and acting next, they could only shrug their shoulders. For even men like this, who had direct access to the Party centre and as much chance as anyone of influencing its views, felt quite unsure how things might develop and remembered how often their recommendations had been brusquely overruled. Finally, a friend in the Ministry of Culture told me that information and documents were being assembled in his office with a view to stopping the publication of *Literární noviny* by simply cancelling its licence —which is what actually happened half a year later.

All these incidents took place during the spring and early summer of 1967, before the writers assembled for their congress. What happened at the Fourth Congress is familiar to students from the verbatim record published soon after the men who had wanted it kept secret fell from power. But the gathering itself was only part of the confrontation whose crucial battles were fought at two private meetings of the communist delegates to the Congress. It was a characteristic stalinist practice, or malpractice, of the Communist Party to exercise its leading role by undemocratically excluding all non-communists from important negotiations. The rule was that Party members should gather before any democratic meeting to discuss what they were in favour of. This practice had become absurd. Every session of the central committee of the Writers' Union, for example, was now preceded by a meeting of its communist fraction[10a] to discuss whatever was on the agenda. On the following day the selfsame group would foregather with the addition of two non-communists (in the period between the Third and Fourth Writers' Congress these were Miroslav Holub[11] and Alexander Matuška), in the capacity of central committee. If the Party members had managed to get through all the business the day before a lot of time was now saved by telling the two newcomers the outcome and asking for their agreement. If, as was more likely, the work had not been finished, it was continued at the second session after a hurried explanation in the corridor so that the non-communists knew what point had been reached and could join in the rest of the discussion.

In a small body like the Writers' Union committee where everyone knew everyone else pretty well, and a non-communist like Holub often had more left-wing views than many an old-guard Party man, it was possible with a certain wry humour *à la Schweik* to put up with this system. Naturally, if the committee was having a session outside Prague, Holub would travel in the same coach as the others; when the communist faction later had its parley he would wait in the corridor, sit in the restaurant or go for a walk till it was over and he was summoned to join in. Since this was insulting as well as ridiculous, the difficulty was finally overcome in one of two different ways: either Holub and Matuška would be invited to join the communist group or else, if a senior Party official had asked for discussion of some point he regarded as a 'purely Party matter', the central committee would temporarily declare itself to be its own Party fraction. Alternatively, the communists would rule that their own Party session was temporarily a meeting of the whole committee in order that the two non-communists could join in the vote for something which fell into the committee's area of competence though it had already been settled in the preceding, purely communist, debate. Thus it sometimes happened that a colleague who had been called away to the telephone, say, would return to find himself taking part in quite a different gathering than the one he had just left and had to check with his neighbours—if they were not too absorbed in the business—to find out whether he was sitting as a Party member or a committee member.

I remember Karel Ptáčník, at one stormy session of the communist members, trying to summarise what had been agreed up to that point and starting off:

'Our central committee has resolved . . .'

There must have been something wrong with this particular resolution, for at that moment the visiting official from the Ideological Department interrupted him and, to make clear that the Party accepted no responsibility for it, corrected him ironically.

'*Your* central committee, you mean.'

'Well, yes, our central committee. Though in a sense they're both ours.'

It was not for the sake of grotesque scenes like these, underlining how far the concept of the Party's leading role had been pushed, that the central *apparat* insisted on summoning communist faction meetings as prescribed in the Statutes whenever it was judged necessary. These meetings were presided over, in our case, by an official of the Central Committee's Ideological Department delegated to ensure that they went as the higher authorities wished. They were one of the instruments, then, by which the political centre influenced the activities and attitudes of non-Party organisations like the Writers' Union. Whenever the steering bodies of such organisations had ideas different from those of the Party leaders, a resolution would be forced through (after dire warnings about discipline, if necessary) on the lines preferred by the centre regardless even of the opinions of Party members present, which were often ignored. In the end communist writers themselves protested against a system which was not only unethical vis-à-vis non-communists, but limited their own democratic rights by forcing them in many cases to vote contrary to their consciences, not to mention their common sense.

However, on the day before the opening of the Fourth Writers' Congress the Party faction duly convened on instructions from the Party Central Committee. František Havlíček, then head of the Ideological Department, was in the chair and the opening address was made on behalf of the Party Presidium by none other than Jiří Hendrych, member of the Presidium, one of the Party secretaries and, as everyone was aware, the second most powerful man after Novotný in the Party and state hierarchy.

Neither the content nor the tone of Hendrych's speech can have left many people in doubt that the Party had decided, in accordance with the classical rules of tactics, to go on to the offensive. But the threadbare arguments he used, and the scanty facts he quoted to back them up, suggested that for the moment there would only be a single sortie. This was surprising for a man like Hendrych, who was certainly not the most stupid figure in the top ranks of the Party and had shown an ability throughout his career to lend colour and apparent logic to many a lifeless doctrine. Not only was he quick-minded and flexible but he was by no means an extreme conservative. His methods were not limited to giving out orders and prohibitions and, as the Party Secretary responsible for art, science, education and propaganda, fields in which few people swallowed the official hard line anyway, he was proud of his reputation as a relatively 'liberal' official who could be swayed by reason. On this occasion, however, he had evidently been allowed no latitude; he was there to present the line as laid down primarily, perhaps entirely, by Comrade Number One himself.

The general section of Hendrych's address contained nothing new. There were the usual pompous assurances of the Party's concern for art and literature, somewhat nostalgic references to the unity of the political and cultural *avant-garde* and conventional assertions that the people, absorbed as it was in the great mission of building a new society, needed a socialist *engagé* literature to inspire and refine it. Each of us, on or off the platform that day, had his own notion of what the public was most absorbed in, and more than one definition of *engagé* could have been offered. To the Party centre, socialist literature meant a harmonious chorus in which each voice sang its own part strictly as the choirmaster indicated. Regarding itself as the only possible spokesman of the only possible form of socialism, it required of every author his conspicuous backing and agreement. This given, a certain scope was allowed for what was called 'differentiation', but in practice this seemed to refer only to literary differences. The humiliating role assigned to creative writers was thus that of confirmers and decorators; they were to show their skill in weaving instructive morality tales from the thread of contemporary events, good and bad alike, and it was conceded that these tales might be more effective than the official political slogans; but they had to point in the same direction. This wretched task proved so impossible that in the end almost all the writers, even those most predisposed in the Party's favour, gave it up. Those few who could not see the immorality of the requirement concentrated on making speeches in support of the Party line, for they were quite unable to produce the sort of literature which the doctrine demanded.

There was another side of the coin, however. The demand for a committed socialist literature meant that anything at all different from this, let alone opposed to it, was attacked and prohibited. Our literature naturally reflected the unadmitted crisis of our society in a world full of conflict. Allegorical statements describing reality in a secret code of vague hints and absurdities— these were tolerated, albeit with no enthusiasm. But any overt discussion or documentary evidence was denounced as hostile thinking. The most genuinely committed authors were pilloried as enemies of socialism, however truly socialist they yearned to be. The suppression of the really *engagé* by the bogus *engagé* acquired dimensions easier to indicate by saying what was *not* published than by attempting a list of prohibited manuscripts. No documentary works, for example, were written; despite the wealth of material for such treatment during the past thirty years of our history, hardly a single eyewitness account of events, hardly a single volume of memoirs or descriptions of trials, political or criminal, appeared on the market. Apart from ephemeral essays reflecting the official prejudice of the day, virtually no books were published in which there was evidence of *thinking*, especially political thinking. It was the very literature of political commitment that was hit hardest by this state of affairs and it is a near-miracle that in the last year or two some books and films appeared which took a broader view of reality, made more comprehensive statements about the society of their time and posed questions of general human import. In every case these works came into being against the wishes of the Party centre and owed their publication either to the cunning or obstinacy of their sponsors or to a momentary weakness, or failure of comprehension, on the part of the licensing authorities.

For Jiří Hendrych, then, to plead on behalf of the Party centre responsible for these perversities in favour of more committed and 'deeply human' writing was not a happy choice. If some optimists had hoped for signs of *détente* from this Congress, or at least for an agreement on the rules of the game as between writers and rulers, then they had already learnt from a source better informed than almost any other that all such prospects were dead and that the rift was getting wider and deeper. How else could one interpret his talk of all-out support for committed literature when it was quite clear what lifeless specimens he had in mind? He spoke of the unprecedented scope for original creation, but the audience knew very well what sort of originality he proposed to reward and how little improvement could be expected in the official attitude to all those creative writers who had been penalised and silenced for wanting to say things in their own way. The man addressing us from the platform enjoyed a position of power and his reasoning was coldly attuned to that fact; if he promised authors a rosy future, he certainly meant it, but only if they supported 'us', as he put it. And 'us' meant the spokesmen of stalinist socialism who had brought the country into its present plight but did not intend to resign office or even rectify their policies.

Even in that purely communist gathering there were many who were shocked by Hendrych's line and felt it to be a scandalous attempt to bribe writers into collaboration. 'Accept our conditions, or else . . .'

One could see the 'or else' round the corner. Orthodox speeches in those days had a standard pattern which no rhetorical skill could disguise. With deadening regularity the first few paragraphs would outline the basis on which co-operation with the authorities would be welcome and advantageous to all. But since this always offered a very narrow platform, incompatible with current thinking and with the real state of affairs anyway, it would be quickly followed by warnings and overt or covert threats of denunciation and prosecution culminating in those sturdy phrases that then ranked as the acme of political wisdom: *We* shall not allow this, *We* shall not permit that. All of which was asserted in the name of the working class, which suffered most from the system of bureaucratic power. The workers had their spokesmen to thank for any odium that they attracted from the rest of society.

The Party's decision to pursue a hard line could also be inferred from its tactical preferences. If it was now applauding what it called socialist literature as the 'honest and realistic stream of writing', then it had clearly decided that the writers who perpetrated it were only temporarily abashed and could, with a suitable combination of political, economic and administrative stimuli, be brought back into the forefront of the cultural world. The same assessment of the situation had evidently brought the Party centre to regard all the other writers as a bunch of anti-socialist pretenders who had usurped authority for a while. Lacking objective criteria and accustomed to judge others by its own psychology and standards of behaviour, the top men in the Party had decided that their critics were their enemies, advocacy of any policy but theirs a base plot, and intellectual debate a crude power struggle. Bemused by its own years of propaganda against the critical thinking in the pages of *Literární noviny*, the

Party centre had come to attribute almost demonic power to the paper, seeing it as the main obstacle to its own untrammelled exercise of authority and making its overthrow a matter of prestige.

I pricked up my ears at the point in Hendrych's speech where the anticipated attack on *Literární noviny* began. He had had had nothing to say about the finer points of cultural policy. He had wasted no time on literary theory or quasi-theoretical polemics: all that had been said many times before and a cross-reference to previous statements was enough. Now was the moment for the attack direct, and Hendrych had chosen what he thought the safest terrain: it was to be a purely political attack.

The Writers' Congress was meeting, as it happened, during those hot June days of 1967 when the Arab-Israeli war had set the world on edge. Our official attitude is well remembered. The Czechoslovak government had immediately followed the Soviets in declaring Israel the aggressor and cutting off diplomatic relations with her. To do so was doubtless the inalienable right of any state. But the brusque and one-sided tone of Czechoslovak propaganda caused embarrassment and distress. Our public had been left uninformed by the domestic press of the complex background to the conflict, in which the paradoxes and injustices of history had been repeated once more; it was not even told about the objective causes of the immediate crisis and the events which had so suddenly culminated in war. The unqualified denunciations of the Israeli attack took no account of the preceding closure of the Persian Gulf by the Arabs and the threat this meant for Israel's national interests and the survival of her people. Israeli policy was painstakingly examined to expose every real or fancied connection with the American leadership, while no effort was made by our press, radio or television to point out the extreme character of official Arab nationalism with its demands for the liquidation of Israel and the Israelis—even though realistically-minded Arabs were later to deplore such fanaticism themselves.

The official Czechoslovak line was purveyed by some of our papers with such exaggerated and frantic zeal that readers were reminded embarrassingly of the campaigns of hatred that accompanied the political trials of the 'fifties, or even the boorish anti-semitism of the Nazi era. There was one Arab diplomat in

Prague who took it upon himself to award marks to our various newspapers according to their competence in applying his own suggestions for hotting up the campaign. In any sovereign state the public is liable to react against such interference by going to the other extreme and indeed it was the crudity and obscurantism of the official position which drove popular sympathy further into the pro-Israeli camp than would normally have been the case. This was shown later when the government campaign was moderated and our press started to carry more serious analyses and commentaries on the complexity of the issues.

Before that stage had been reached, *Literární noviny* decided to publish a symposium featuring the views of four writers who had recently visited both sides in the conflict. Oldřich Daněk, Jan Procházka, [12] Arnošt Lustig[12] and Ivan Klíma were the protagonists in the discussion. Each of them described his experiences in Israel and the U.A.R. Little was said about the war itself but much about its historical, social and psychological background as well as about the traditions and atmosphere of the two countries generally. The talk ranged over such themes as the *kibbutzim*; the Arab hostility to Britain since colonial times, which gave them some common ground with Germany; and the accidental but none the less dangerous connection between anti-semitism in Germany and in the Arab lands.

Today such a symposium could appear in any Czech paper, even the Party daily *Rudé právo*, without arousing alarm or perhaps even much attention. At that time, however, since the editors of *Literární noviny* were anxious to avoid causing further friction between the Party centre and the relatively independent journals, they sent a transcript of the discussion to the 'Central Publications Board' (i.e. the censor) with a request for an advisory opinion about how it could be published, what changes might be necessary and in what form it could appear. Far from giving its opinion the Board promptly classified the transcript as confiscated (or suspended, to use the formula of that time) which meant that a summary, or quotations, or even the entire text would be sent in a special bulletin to all members of the Party Presidium and Secretariat, certain ministers and other select officials.

There was an amusing sequel to this side of the story. While this was going on Oldřich Daněk, for reasons that had to be respected, changed his mind about the symposium and asked *Literární noviny* not to publish his contributions. The cut text never appeared in *Literární noviny* anyway because of the censor's veto, but one version turned up later in a West German newspaper after the writers' quarrel with the Party leadership had become a front-page story in the West. The suspicion was immediately aroused that *Literární noviny* had sent it to the Germans—a discovery that would have delighted those who were for ever seeking evidence of secret links in that direction. The theory, however, was fortunately disproved on the spot, for the German version included the comments by Daněk which had never been reproduced except in the censor's bulletin with its very restricted circulation. I cannot say with what intensity the search for a 'secret link' continued after that; it might, after all, have led to disclosures far more sensational than anything concerning *Literární noviny*.

It was the transcript of the Middle East symposium, however, which was now used by Hendrych as a stick with which to beat the political views of our paper. Up to this point he had been reading unemotionally enough from his script, concentrating on diction rather than effect. True, it was a hot day for histrionics, but we are speaking of a part of Europe where orators normally adhere to the written word in any case. As soon as he came to mention *Literární noviny*, however, Hendrych's delivery changed; his manner became more dramatic and he started to improvise whole passages. His indignation, it was apparent, did not all derive from official policy; he was speaking from conviction.

He was shocked, he said, that our journal had passed from the stage of prejudice and apathy to direct and undisguised attacks on the state and Party. (Thus he described the very mild criticism we had made of certain decisions and practices of the Party centre.) *Literární noviny*, he declared, was in danger of becoming an outright opposition paper and the measures previously taken to correct this trend had been far too half-hearted. Hendrych went on to congratulate the censorship on suppressing certain critical articles; indeed, the need for a censor's office to protect the country and the Party would clearly remain as long as papers like ours were run by such irresponsible characters—or was it sheer ill-will?

We have been too patient for too long, Hendrych said in conclusion to this part of his address. We have been content to
persuade and warn, hoping that the writers would put their own
house in order. In its public opinion polls, its symposia and its
readers' columns *Literární noviny* has now transgressed the limits
of any decent debate. The time has come to rally to the defence of
the Republic.

This was more than a final warning; it was an ultimatum. It
was also the core of Hendrych's whole address and an implicit
answer to the question, what did the Party expect of the Congress.
The answer was simply this: if the Congress failed to call the
paper to heel, the Party centre would intervene over the head of
the Writers' Union. The tone was now set for the rest of the
Congress, moreover; Hendrych's remarks had the effect of
virtually catapulting many of the delegates out of their seats and
up on to the speakers' dias.

I cannot judge whether or not, for the purposes which the
Party centre had set itself, this aggressive opening move was a
wise one. But the Congress was only one detail in a more protracted conflict. The Party centre had the option of conceding
some of the writers' demands and continuing the ding-dong
battle which had driven it on to the defensive, or of rejecting
them entirely and intimidating the enemy with a view to his total
defeat. Whatever the Party's decision at the general strategic
level, in its confrontation with the writers Hendrych's speech was
a foretaste of the latter line.

The Party centre's spokesman, then, had started off by touching
upon two of the sorest points of public policy—the censorship
and the Arab-Israeli war. Perhaps he had chosen the second
subject so that his attack on *Literární noviny* should not appear too
narrowly concerned with the current criticisms of Czechoslovak
Party policy. However, it was a weapon that turned against him.
The questions concerning *Literární noviny* were promptly pushed
into the background amid a surge of criticism directed at the
Party centre's whole political method and morality. Hendrych
and his assistants found themselves at bay. Unaccustomed to
hearing official standpoints argued with or even questioned in
open debate, they felt their standing as apostles of the truth
gravely damaged. It was a painful blow to their self-esteem.

The next speaker on the list was Jiří Šotola, who was both the outgoing first secretary of the Writers' Union and the outgoing editor-in-chief of its journal. The juxtaposition was pure chance: Šotola had put his name down to speak before Hendrych delivered his address, and had prepared a script at home. Now that he realised what effect it would have, he felt ill at ease. A quiet man, for whom life's conflicts held no secret at other levels, he hated the noise of political strife. Nevertheless he rose, took a deep breath and began.

Where Hendrych had quoted a single example of the beneficial effect, as he saw it, of censorship, Šotola quoted dozens of cases of interference by the censor with *Literární noviny*, all designed to suppress views which only the most hidebound mind could call 'anti-socialist' or to prevent criticism in an age when even the Party centre theoretically regarded critics as a 'motive force of society'. (In practice, alas, all they set in motion was the rotary presses in the censor's office.) Šotola made no drama of it, offered no comment. He merely gave a report on the true state of affairs, and that was eloquent enough.

There was a hush in the hall when he finished. The book-writers in the audience had had their taste of the censor too, but newspapers were far worse afflicted than novels and Šotola's dry account was an eye-opener for many Party members present.

I am not sure if it was exactly at this point that the current chief censor, Colonel E. Kovařík, began to run confusedly around the corridors from one Union official to another, protesting excitedly at what he called 'the witchhunt'. By this he referred not to the persecution of writers, but to the exposure of the censors. Later on I had several occasions to watch him bobbing around and could only marvel at his vitality. No doubt he owed it to the fear of being deservedly pinpointed as chief witch himself.

However, the scene was now set for a more wide-ranging confrontation at the Congress between the agents of the Party centre and the rebellious writers. Further delegates had already asked to speak, incensed by Hendrych's ill-tempered and ill-reasoned defence of the official line on the Middle East. It might have been more merciful to forget it, but as things were Hendrych had started a debate. And it only took place at the Writers' Congress because, in those days, it could not conceivably take place in parliament, in the press, on radio or television or at public meetings of any kind.

Since Hendrych had only brought in the Middle East as a stick to beat *Literární noviny* with, it was ironical that the man to answer him was a writer whom no one would have dreamed of associating with any inner or outer circle around that paper. This was Arnošt Lustig, one of the participants in the notorious symposium. He started by saying quite openly what had been on everyone's mind: that in comparison with the Arab-Israeli issue the argument over *Literární noviny* was quite secondary. To concentrate on the latter could only be a deliberate attempt to distract attention from the former, that is from the unjust, mendacious and dangerous official line and the unscrupulous attitude to the Party and the public shown by those who followed it.

His own fate and the fate of those close to him have made Arnošt Lustig uncommonly sensitive to the everyday injustices, deliberate and otherwise, inflicted on the unfortunate Jewish minority by their fellow-citizens. The thought of them endows him moreover with a marvellous eloquence, beside which his opponent's arguments sound like the stuttering of a nervous schoolchild. The way he took up the cudgels for *Literární noviny* swept the complaints against it into limbo, even though it was not the paper that concerned him at all. The four-man discussion of the Arab-Israeli question, he exclaimed, was no anti-Party plot by *Literární noviny*, for it was he, Lustig, who had suggested it and forced the idea through despite the editors' lamentations that it would never work and would only cause trouble and recriminations. It made him despair as a communist and a citizen of a socialist state that *Rudé právo* should adopt the same tone as those anti-semitic Nazi propaganda-sheets which paved the way to the gas-chambers of Auschwitz and helped to salve the consciences of the public. He felt an urge and a duty to warn the leaders of state and Party against the dangers of this path. Yet he had not been able to approach a single senior official to give him the straight opinion of a man-in-the-street and rank-and-file Party member. They were always too busy. So he and Luděk Pachmann and Jan Procházka had written a joint letter to Jiří Hendrych. But it had remained unanswered. (On a later occasion when Hendrych was to discuss the Congress and the Middle East with

Procházka, and was reminded of this letter, he cut him short with 'Don't start poking your nose into politics or we'll stamp on your toes!')

'So I chose the only other possible way of getting my views noticed by the leading men and warning them,' Lustig went on. 'And that was the *Literární noviny* symposium. I knew the censor would confiscate the text, but that was my method of making sure all the competent officials would get copies on their desk and read what I had to tell them.'

How exactly Lustig's plan had fulfilled his expectations was meanwhile apparent to everyone: Hendrych's speech had itself been ample testimony. Though there were a number of such incidents at the communist fraction meeting that showed how wide a gulf now separated most of the Party writers from the *apparat*, when he came to wind up the session František Havlíček spoke from the chair as if nothing had gone amiss and Hendrych's exposition had won general acclaim. The spokesmen of the *apparat* made no reference of any kind to the many serious criticisms that had been raised, though they must have realised they were outnumbered, not to say isolated. They maintained a contemptuous attitude not only towards the writers as such, but towards all rank-and-file opinion in their own Party. By 'putting principle first' they meant having their own way even if it was no one else's, and whenever they had exhausted the possibilities of outmanœuvring and intimidating people they were quite prepared to use force. As they truthfully said, they hated to do this. But only because it chipped their images as self-styled protectors of the public interest.

Still, it seemed that the Party centre did not yet regard the possibilities of manœuvring as exhausted. Perhaps it was simply that it had not yet had time to digest the communist fraction meeting and was still proceeding according to Plan A. Or perhaps it hoped that the storm would blow over and that after the initial tantrums, only to be expected at a meeting of literary men, there would follow the equally normal effort of the 'moderate wing' to accept the adamant demands of the authorities. The authorities, after all, held all the reins of financial and publishing policy in their hands; they were in a position to influence not only what the writers wrote, but how much they ate.

Particular interest attaches, then, to one of the numerous proposals tabled to modify the list of candidates for election to the new central committee of the Writers' Union. This was a proposal concerning not who should be *on* the committee, but who should be *off* it. A draft list of the next committee had already been prepared by the outgoing one and approved, in the usual way, by its communist fraction. This draft was now up for discussion by the communist delegates of the Congress itself, whose meeting had dragged on late into the night. The visiting spokesmen for the Party centre did not yet think it advisable or perhaps even tactful to come straight out with names of who should be on the new writers' committee. Through semi-private contacts and quiet lobbying, however, they had already started a campaign against having anyone from the staff of *Literární noviny*, or close to the paper. They whispered that so-and-so was a mediocre writer of much-inflated reputation, while such-and-such was a mere translator, of whom there were too many in the committee anyway. All Jiří Hendrych had said publicly in this connection was that it would not do for the supreme body in the Writers' Union to include anyone who was 'ideologically confused', while the sort of people who should be strongly represented were the 'realist' novelists of the older and middle generations. In official language, however, this was merely a euphemism for politically pliable authors who might have produced creditable work in their younger days.

When one of the Party writers, then, who was known to have close contacts with the *apparat*, now rose and with obviously mixed feelings asked for the removal of three names—Milan Jungmann, Ivan Klíma and Ludvík Vaculík—from the approved committee list, it was obvious on whose behalf he was acting. The plan to use the Congress for an assault on *Literární noviny* and for an attempt, perhaps a final attempt, to use the Writers' Union as a means of seizing the paper from within, came out into the open again. The Party centre, still anxious to hide its hand, now indulged in an elegant and much-favoured variant of the tactic known as vicarious struggle. In this case the protagonist did appear at first glance to be fighting his own fight, but any close observer must have discovered that he was propelled from elsewhere. Pavel Hanuš further disgraced himself by muddling his brief. He described Jungmann as a member of the Party Central Committee by virtue of his post in the *Literární noviny* office, which he had long since resigned; of Vaculík he said he had nothing against him, but he had been too short a time in the Union; as for Klíma, he objected to his statements in the Union's central committee and behind the scenes. Asked by Klíma to substantiate this charge of intriguing, he asked for ten minutes to reconsider; after a little while he produced a revised version of his comment on Klíma, with the reference to activity 'behind the scenes' left out.

A secret ballot was then held and the list of names as submitted by the writers' committee approved with a single change. Votes were next taken on each name separately and on all other proposals and counter-proposals. The outcome was that the only name on the draft list not to be confirmed was that of Ivan Skála, not a man associated with *Literární noviny* but on the contrary an editor of the Party daily *Rudé právo*, a member of the Party Central Committee, a National Assembly deputy and a staunch supporter of the Party centre of his day. The name voted in by the communist delegates to replace Skála's was that of Pavel Kohout.

(It did not stay on the list for long. After the two opening days of the Congress the same communist faction met again and struck off the list four names this time: Klíma, Vaculík, Havel, Kohout. But by that time the atmosphere was quite different. The faction's second meeting was short and practically devoid of talk. Jiří Hendrych appeared armed with an undisguised Party order and backed it not only by invoking Party discipline but by threatening the very existence of the Writers' Union.)

3
The Congress opens

On the day after the first stormy meeting of the communist fraction the Congress proper began. Its opening marked a further worsening of relations between the Party leaders and the majority of writers, now all assembled in one place. After Vilem Závada's word of welcome Milan Kundera[13] took the floor and briefly introduced a Draft Statement of the Writers' Standpoint, an attempt to review the role of literature in the wider context of our national and state history. Every delegate was given a text of the Draft Statement, which had already been approved by the Union's central committee. This procedure implied deliberate abandonment, as Kundera explained, of the traditional type of opening report with its questionable and quickly outdated official assessments in favour of the more difficult task of making possible a really free exchange of views among all who wished to speak.

This attempt to break free from the stereotyped pattern of the conventional Congress with its inevitable stalinist atmosphere was greatly objected to at the time in certain circles, though several other organisations have made similar efforts to introduce some serious intellectual work into their annual foregatherings. Kundera's repudiation of the stalinist technique of stage-management was regarded as an insolent bid to give the Congress a new character—the character which in fact it speedily acquired.

What shocked the orthodox most in Kundera's behaviour, however, was that having briefly referred to the Draft Statement he proceeded to add his own gloss to it in a speech denouncing all the ossified concepts of stalinism and offering a new view, based on historical analysis, and depicting the political zealots of the day as a menace to the national interest. Kundera's essay was later represented as a great political scandal, though to anyone who heard or read it it must have been clear that it was designed to provoke serious thought.

After Kundera's performance the next address, by Jiří Hendrych, fell flat indeed. It was later suggested, indeed, that the juxtaposition was a piece of deliberate malice by the 'managers'. All the same, it is hard to believe that any other sequence would have enhanced the effect of Hendrych's contribution. Far be it from me to make a straight comparison between Kundera and Hendrych as orators. The fact is that the intellectual sterility of the Party line in those days prevented its spokesman from departing from their platitudinous, collectively prefabricated scripts. It is no wonder that their style was as unimpressive as their content was contemptible.

The speech that now followed linked on to the previous night's Party discussion and acquired a more dramatic setting than its author had ever intended. Once more the hidden hand of an 'organiser' was descried in this—an unknown and indeed impossible personage, able somehow to persuade as motley a bunch of personalities as the writers of Czechoslovakia to stand up and speak according to some prearranged schedule and on prearranged lines. It would be more to the point to suggest that if Hendrych himself had not presented such an aggressively one-sided version of the Arab-Israeli conflict and had done no more than admit the complexity of the issues and his own difficulty as an official spokesman in publicly stating the doubts that he probably felt, then Pavel Kohout's contribution would have passed off with much less commotion.

As it was, however, Kohout found himself on the platform graphically describing how for many years a certain powerful state had threatened its small neighbour with destruction. He did not name the countries but it was clear that he had the Middle East in mind, and clear too that the protagonists could equally well have been Nazi Germany and the Czechoslovak Republic. Then came the rhetorical question: If we had summoned up courage and actively defended ourselves, instead of passively awaiting to be attacked, how would we then have felt if the world had dubbed us the aggressor? If Kohout's parable seemed like a gesture of defiance and contempt, it was less to the credit of the speaker (let alone the stage-managers) than to the previous efforts of the Party mouthpieces.

Now came Alexander Kliment with a comment stressing the ethical issues. He ended his series of criticisms and suggestions with a proposal that was to have enormous impact because of the official reaction to it. He requested simply that the secretariat of the Writers' Union should take steps to keep members better informed; it was embarrassing, for example, that they should have to find out about important literary events from *Le Monde* or the West German radio. He had in mind, he explained, such cases as Alexander Solzhenitsyn's letter to the Fourth Congress of Soviet Writers. 'I propose,' Kliment ended, 'that our Congress be made familiar with this letter. And since I myself know what is in it, I hereby express my solidarity with its author.'

Before the applause had died away Pavel Kohout was on his feet. 'I have a Czech translation of the Solzhenitsyn letter here. Does the Congress wish to know what it says?'

Another spontaneous burst of clapping provided the answer. But the chairman, Karel Ptáčník, being a conscientious official with a deep sense of propriety inculcated, perhaps, during his years of office on the local National Committee in Bruntál, insisted on a vote. It was taken: one against, two abstained.

As Kohout advanced to the platform the indignation of Jiří Hendrych, who had been seething throughout the afternoon, finally boiled over. While Kohout read the opening words of the letter Hendrych rose, put on the jacket he had doffed in the heat, picked up his brief-case and walked out. As he passed the back row of chairs on the platform where Kundera, Procházka and Lustig were sitting he paused just long enough to say to them:

'You have lost everything, absolutely everything.'

After this ostentatious exit, which was destined to have far-reaching consequences, one or two of the audience who knew Hendrych personally ran after him to try and dissuade him from breaking relations with the Congress, but failed to make any impression. Outside in the foyer Hendrych had already been buttonholed by a veteran bard, Karel Šelepa, who had long since ceased to concern himself with current affairs and was trying to impress the chief ideologist of the need to change the text of the national anthem and replace it, perhaps, with some verses he happened to have composed himself.

Šelepa was probably the only man in the building at that moment whose mind was not on the Solzhenitsyn letter. It will be recalled that this letter had not even been read out at the Soviet Writers' Congress to which it was originally addressed. The Russian author, whose unique and masterly depiction of Stalin's labour camps in *One Day in the Life of Ivan Denisovich* had brought him world fame overnight, had protested in this letter against the oppressiveness of a censorship which made it impossible for him to continue his own work. He had described the damage done to Soviet literature by Stalin's purges and the way in which the survivors, prevented from telling the tale, had to see their own writings hacked about as well. With truly Russian pathos he denounced the arbitrary rule of the censor, who not only stopped the publication of what had been written but prevented the writing of what had been genuinely observed and felt, prevented talent from developing or, if it developed, from being seen and recognised. He had quoted his own wretched experience, listed the works he had been forbidden to publish and asked his own Union, instead of acting as the extended arm of the bureaucracy, to revolt against such practices and stand up for artistic and civic rights.

I happened to have been in Moscow with a small group of writers at the time when the Soviet Congress was held and had seen the extreme reactions on either side that the Solzhenitsyn letter provoked. The leaders of the Soviet Writers' Union, who had been bitterly attacked in it, reacted with equal severity and declared it, in tune with the official denunciations, to be prejudiced, untrue and libellous. Accordingly they would not allow it to be read out, let alone debated, at their own gathering. Many of the Soviet writers, however, took the view that a man of Solzhenitsyn's standing ought to be given a hearing and that there were many valuable points in his letter that needed discussing, even if not all the charges were quite accurate.

I had managed to get hold of a copy of the letter in Moscow and was amazed to see how closely its contents reflected our own problems (though the writer, without regard to his own safety, had expressed himself in language caustic and melancholy by turns, utterly different from our own sober way). I was not to know that only a few days later, at our own Writers' Congress, I should be hearing a similar protest from someone who could not have read the Russian one, namely the Slovak poet Laco Novomeský.[14] There were the same arguments, rising above the everyday vices of censorship to the general issues of the growth of national culture. There was the same nobility of mind. Only Solzhenitsyn's anger was missing, to be replaced by a sad wisdom bred of the awareness of infinity and the knowledge that all problems will be solved tomorrow if not today. Solved, perhaps, when we are no longer here to witness it.

When I started to show Solzhenitsyn's letter to my colleagues in the aircraft flying back to Prague it turned out that nearly all of them had seen it, and had copies in their pockets too. Its distribution had been attended to in Moscow by that institution known as *samizdat*, or publish-it-yourself, in which carbon paper replaces the printing press and personal friendship the book trade. There were many Soviet authors who, failing to get Solzhenitsyn's letter read at their Congress, felt it their duty to ensure its publication abroad as one way of trying to mitigate Solzhenitsyn's own tragic fate as well as bringing home to their own officials the urgency of the problems of literary production and censorship. In this way his letter appeared in *Le Monde* and thereafter in other papers throughout the world, no doubt receiving more publicity than if it had been handled by the Soviet Writers' Congress and the Soviet press as its author intended.

As we flew back from Moscow with Solzhenitsyn's text we all pondered over the problem of how he could be helped, and over the equally oppressive issue of censorship as we had come to know it ourselves. I mention this because of the subsequent story of Kohout slyly procuring the text and irrelevantly bringing it into our own Congress so as to influence it improperly. If we had had no censorship in our country, or one restricted to the guarding of military and state secrets (which in fact fell outside our censors' competence altogether), the whole question would never have arisen and Kohout would have had no motive to produce the letter. But as it was we not only needed to express our sympathy with Solzhenitsyn and, if possible, to help him, we also found the letter a moving expression of problems we had in common. Dozens of our writers had read the letter before our own Congress began and if Pavel Kohout had not read it out there I am sure someone else would have done before the meeting ended.

However, this did not prevent certain members of the Party *apparat*, along with a number of writers, from later exercising their ingenuity by describing how Kliment and Kohout—who in fact hardly knew each other and had very dissimilar views and interests—had cunningly arranged things between them. Later on I tried to argue some of these officials out of their obsession and, failing that, to bring them round a table with the two 'conspirators'—but it was hopeless.

After my return from Moscow a small group of us met, as was our pleasant habit when one of us had been abroad, to exchange impressions. This time the rendezvous was at Kliment's, where we cooked ourselves Russian-style borshch and chatted more about Soviet Central Asia (which I had just visited) than about the impending Writers' Congress. Among other friends present, unsurprisingly, were Ivan Klíma and Ludvík Vaculík, later to be branded as the Congress's chief conspirators contrary to all probability: no one who knew them at all would find the suggestion other than risible. In fact I had brought the Solzhenitsyn letter along with me and before we looked at it I mentioned how it had impressed me and said I should like to read it out at the Congress. At first the idea appealed to the company, but in the end we agreed that it would be unhelpful in the circumstances. We considered how ultra-sensitive the Soviet authorities were to anything they considered interference in their own affairs; we thought of the special relationship between the Soviet Union and our own Party leaders, who would no doubt accuse the entire literary community of trying to complicate life for them. As long as the state of chronic tension between our writers and our rulers continued, we said to ourselves, we should not risk making matters even worse and lose the chance of reaching useful working agreements at the Congress. Finally, it struck us that we might make things worse rather than better for Solzhenitsyn himself. (We did not yet know about the publication of his letter in *Le Monde*, which occurred about this time.)

Our discussion, of course, was a great deal more agitated than I have suggested in this summary of the conclusions we reached; I merely offer it as further evidence that Alexander Kliment could not have had any prior agreement with Pavel Kohout about reading the letter at the Congress.

The charge of 'conspiracy' was in any case grotesque. The letter was read simply because the grievances and the reactions they met with in Russia strongly resembled those in Czecho-slovakia. If this similarity was so close, the fault lay not with those who were charged with conspiracy but with those who laid the charge.

Again, there could hardly have been a more vivid illustration of the absurdity of the situation than the threat to create a national, nay, an international incident out of the publicity given to a literary document at a *closed* meeting. Granted that the real relationship between the two countries involved made any reading of the Solzhenitsyn letter likely to be interpreted as provocative, there were plenty of respectable ways of preventing a scandal. The letter could have been cyclostyled and included in the dossiers for the information of delegates. If it were thought undesirable to have it put out in the open press, it could have been published in the Union's internal bulletin, or a notice issued envisaging publication later. If those who were so opposed to the public reading had not so completely abandoned the art of political persuasion in preference for issuing straight instructions, they could have addressed the delegates as soon as the proposal was made, asked them to abandon it and explained how damaging it would be to our relations with the U.S.S.R. They would cer-tainly have found an understanding audience if they had then added that they had no wish to withhold information and would ensure that all members of the Union received copies through internal channels shortly. The delegates would not then, I am sure, have insisted on the letter being read aloud, for they had no illusions about the relations of 'equality' prevailing among the socialist countries.

The men who counted in the Party, however, had long since given up open policy-making and were accustomed to having their way by issuing 'directives' and enunciating 'themes' already agreed on within the narrow forum of the Party centre, where democratic discussion was regarded either as a hindrance or a menace. Hendrych's remark 'You have lost everything!' and his dramatic exit from the hall boded ill, then. Every attempt to build a diplomatic bridge over which he could peacefully return to the Congress proved vain. When he did finally come back, two days later, he was in full armour.

The first and most important gesture of conciliation was made, shortly after Hendrych disappeared, by Professor Eduard Goldstücker.[6] His approach was a model which the other side might well have copied if it had not succumbed completely to authoritarian techniques. 'This letter,' began the professor,

> was evidently already known from various sources to the great majority of those present and has represented something of a public secret at our Congress. The request was put to the chair, as you heard, for the letter to be read aloud. The Congress agreed, the chairman (I am told) received a proposal on these lines in writing, and the letter was read out. I think it is important to appreciate that this is a matter of concern to the Soviet Writers' Union and we should remain faithful to a principle we loudly quote when our own affairs are involved, namely that as friends from different socialist countries we should not criticise one another within our respective professional spheres. We insisted on this principle when our friends made public criticism of our own cultural policies. If we want this principle applied to ourselves we must respect it where our friends are concerned. I therefore propose that the reading of the letter by A. Solzhenitsyn should be regarded as an act of internal information within this Congress, should not appear in the records and should not be referred to in further discussion.

This argument was accepted and acted upon. But Goldstücker's diplomatic success in whisking the Solzhenitsyn letter out of existence for international purposes did not mean that it had ceased to exist in that small territory enclosed between the Czechoslovak Writers' Union and the Secretariat of the Czechoslovak Communist Party, especially not in that most exposed portion of the territory, the broken-down building at No. 1

Betlemská Street, where *Literární noviny* had its office. Here the repercussions of the reading continued unabated. The search for evil motives behind the Congress grew more frantic. Some of the more uncontrollable members of the Party *apparat* begin to behave like amateur detectives, fitting the facts to suit their preconceived theories with the cavalier impatience of sleuths about to pounce on their prey. Kliment, for example, was suddenly described as an editor of the paper though he had merely contributed to it and held a part-time post in the editorial office for a few months. It became plain that whatever happened at the Congress contrary to the Party centre's wishes would be used as new evidence that a small group of people connected with *Literární noviny* were at the bottom of it all. The logical deduction from this theory was that the group must be exposed and isolated, and then driven out by the writers themselves from their lairs in the central committee of the Union and the offices of its weekly paper.

From this point on, anyone able to observe the Congress and the second Communist faction meeting, with their various demands and resolutions, internal Party reports and disciplinary measures, would be forced to conclude that there was, after all, a secret scenario. But it was the men who had been most indignant in complaining of the imaginary 'stage-managers' behind the first part of the Congress who were now to insist most frantically, though ineffectually, on strict adherence to their own scripts and timetables. Of course they had never objected to meetings being organised; only to their being organised by other people. With what shameless enthusiasm they had applied themselves in the past to stage-managing dozens of congresses, conferences and meetings of all kinds! Were we to think they had lost the knack when it came to the Fourth Writers' Congress? Clearly they had not forgotten the technique. It was just that, in this case, the technique failed to work.

Understandably enough, they sought the failure of their own organisational effort in the existence of some counter-organisation, for they attributed to the other side the practices which they had grown accustomed to indulge in, and rely upon, themselves. It was evidently beyond their power to conceive of any cause of failure springing from the objective state of society and the reflection of that society in the minds of men of letters. It could not be expected that they should see horizons obscured for them by the blueprints of stalinist thinking, or that they should entertain the notion that their behaviour might be wrong and their 'leading role' unjustified. There have, after all, been systems far more enlightened than Stalin's which imposed the same mental limitations on their supporters.

The rest of the Congress and its consequences can only be understood on the assumption of some such predetermined scenario in the minds of the Party stalwarts. If we consider the actual speeches made by one or two of the writers who had been convicted in advance by the secret index, the absurdity of the whole situation, and of their individual positions, becomes quite apparent. There were to be two more important contributions to the debate on censorship: one by Laco Novomeský who was too ill to attend, so that Vojtech Mihálik read it for him, and the other by Ivan Klíma. The basic ideas and drift of the two speeches were very similar. Klíma must have irritated the authorities by the sharp edge of his polemical wit and by the irony he used in demonstrating that our present rulers, far from advancing our freedom of expression, have thrown us back into a worse state than we knew as part of Austria-Hungary a century ago. Novomeský's address, though on a more general plane of thought, could hardly have been any more acceptable to the Party pundits. Yet the reaction to it was merely a restrained distaste, as of men resolved to suppress its dangerous thoughts quietly some other time; Klíma's speech, by contrast, was immediately labelled anti-Party and well-nigh anti-state, though anyone re-reading it must marvel at this choice of epithets. As I told Klíma later, he might as well have stood up on the platform and sung the *Internationale*: they would still have expelled him from the Party. Whence the different treatment? It was not just Novomeský's unique poetic and moral stature and the fact that he spent tragic years in a stalinist gaol. What also counted was that Klíma was a leading figure on the editorial board of *Literární noviny*.

There were several speakers at the Congress who discussed the inadequacies of the Party's cultural policy and tried to suggest better guidelines for it: Milan Kundera, Eduard Goldstücker, Václav Havel,[3] Milan Jungmann and Lumír Čivrný amongst them. They all had a cold reception but in no case were their views promptly attacked as 'anti-Party'. This is precisely what happened, however, to A. J. Liehm, though his thinking was clearly more deeply rooted in socialism than that of several other delegates who addressed the Congress. Liehm, like Klíma, was evidently on the black list and had to be put down whatever he said.

Václev Havel concentrated on reviewing the work of the Writers' Union itself. Some of his remarks might have been thought hypercritical by some, but no stretch of the imagination could have made them anti-socialist. He attacked the concept of the Union as a 'transmission belt' for Party policy. But it is hard to see how the strongest critique of an organisation which is in theory non-communist, coming from a man who is himself a non-communist, could be called an attack on the Party. Presumably the Party centre considered that the old differences between Havel and *Literární noviny* had now been so whittled away that if the influence of the paper could be destroyed, the influence of Havel and the literary group around him would die too. The assessment showed at least that both Havel and *Literární noviny* were equally repugnant to the authorities.

In contrast to the speakers already mentioned there were a few who seemed to stand at the opposite pole; either they had been deliberately mustered for the purpose or their remarks fitted conveniently into the Party centre's plan, supplying it with useful arguments and encouraging those few spokesmen who believed their own propaganda and felt themselves to be acting according to the needs and wishes, if not of the writers in general, at least of the 'healthy core' among them.

It is rather odd that the Congress speeches of Alexej Pludek, Oldřich Šuleř, Milan Lajčiak, Jiří Hájek[15] and Ivan Skála contained passages in justification not only of the Party centre's various measures at the Writers' Congress, but also of those which it failed to put through at the time and only carried out later by simply issuing instructions. One of the most tortuous arguments was that of Pludek, who treated Havel and *Literární noviny* as a single category simply because it suited the Party to kill these two different-looking birds with one stone.

Pludek, then, arrayed himself as an isolated non-communist alongside the communists backing the official line. Havel, conversely, found himself though a non-Party man associated with Party members on the critical side. These two exemplified the way in which opinions were divided not along Party lines, but quite athwart them and regardless of philosophical affiliation. The reason for this phenomenon, which was characteristic of public attitudes in our country, was no doubt to be sought partly in the analogous treatment by the Party centre of the public and of its various social components. The centre at that time often relied on the co-operation of heterogenous groups and individuals which tended to be unmilitant and backward in their views, professionally not too competent, and very loosely allied by a common interest in maintaining the power structure from which they all benefited. The more efficient and go-ahead elements of society, on the other hand, since they were alienated and finally persecuted by the Party centre, were drawn together by their common resentment in a unity that was equally superficial in its way.

Stalinist socialism came to favour the conservative and the mediocre everywhere instead of pursuing the ideals of social justice. It would be wrong to concentrate overmuch on those whom the system corrupted, or on those whom it disillusioned after they had sacrificed themselves to their leaders in the honest conviction that they were aiding the progress of socialism, only to realise in the end that they had been hindering it. The greatest damage the system wrought was to the cause itself by disorganising and frustrating the intellectual development of the Left in its search for socialist solutions.

Those writers who, on instructions or out of conviction, supported the centre's line at the Congress and the fraction meetings, were rendering poor service to the socialist cause they proclaimed. Things are admittedly clearer in retrospect, but they did what they did at a time when the lines were already clearly drawn in the literary field and the character of the Party's machinations obvious. If they failed to understand what was happening during the Congress, or shortly after it when some of them received their rewards,* they may at least have realised

* Alexej Pludek, after the Congress, was made chief editor of *belles lettres* in *Práce*, Jiři Hájek was given the corresponding post in the *Svoboda* publishing house, Milan Lajčiak became editor-in-chief of the weekly *Predvoj* and Ivan Skála became an editor of the Mladá fronta publishers.

later when their apologies were a mere superfluous accompaniment to a series of disgracefully repressive acts in which the original clash of opinions was quite forgotten.

The executors of the Party centre's line were meanwhile far more intensively occupied behind the scenes than in public. When the official head of the Party and government delegation to the Congress, Jiří Hendrych, left the hall as we have described, he was followed by every guest who held any high Party or state office. This left some large gaps among the platform seats where at one time, indeed, Juraj Špitzer, Jiří Šotola and Jan Procházka were the only figures to be seen. Down in the hall, however, as well as in the corridors and adjoining offices, dozens of Party Central Committee officials were to be seen along with high dignitaries from the censor's office, representatives of ministries and various institutions, not to mention people whose faces were quite unfamiliar and whose function could only be guessed at. All these guests, invited or otherwise, appeared to be getting a great deal more excitement out of the Congress than the writers themselves. The face that etched itself deepest in my memory belonged to the chief censor, Colonel Kovařík, whose prophetic phrase about 'witch hunts' I have mentioned above. It was evident that he found difficulty in containing himself. The principal editors of *Literární noviny*, as we gathered from colleagues at the Congress, had already been warned by the censor's office that a minimum of publicity was to be accorded to the event. Only Jiří Hendrych's speech was to be fully covered, and anything out of harmony with it was to be suppressed altogether. Some of the correspondents showed us what havoc the censors had already wreaked with the original versions of their own stories to their papers.

The Party's Central Committee officials seemed to be spending their time at the Congress, when not otherwise engaged, spreading gloom about the outcome of it all. It was they who laid the first charges against alleged 'organisers' and 'stage-managers' of various 'attacks on the Party' and warned that nobody should be surprised if the Party replied in kind or even more vigorously. There were many rumours in circulation about what form this vigour might take. Everyone agreed they would affect *Literární noviny* and some thought the Union's publishing house, Československý spisovatel, would be penalised by having its paper supplies cut off or by being simply taken away from the Union and given to the state. This would not only have threatened the livelihood of large numbers of writers but would have undermined the Union's financial independence: till now it had covered its own costs from the fairly large profit it made on publishing books and papers, even if most of that was taken away in taxation.

'They'll stop us publishing and confiscate the *Litfond*'* went the cry.

It was a common reaction to these rumours to suggest that, if *Literární noviny* was to be lost, at least the fund should be clung on to, and it would be dishonest to deny that most of those who reacted in this way were authors themselves. But 'clinging to the fund' would inevitably mean meeting the Party centre half-way. There was therefore a great wave of lobbying and agitating to collect signatures for various petitions and declarations denouncing 'all attacks on the leadership of state or Party' and deploring any 'misuse of the Congress for dishonest political ends'. It is to the writers' credit that they did not sign any of these servile statements in sufficient numbers to cut much ice in the issues at stake. The texts lie forgotten today in the obscurity of secret archives. One such composition was penned by the poet Milan Lajčiak, who read it out from the platform himself:

> In contrast to certain speakers and to that tiny handful who passionately applaud every subtle attack, prepared weeks ago, upon
> 1. the foreign policy of our socialist state and the whole socialist camp,
> 2. the Central Publication Board [i.e. the censors—Author's note],
> 3. Party and state officialdom, and
> 4. the Soviet Union's domestic and foreign policies,

* The *Litfond* (officially, the Czech Literary Fund) was endowed from a two per cent levy on all publisher's payments after deduction of the state tax, which varied from five to thirty per cent according to the amount taxed The fund provided grants for authors at the start of their careers, or engaged on long-term projects.

all in the name of democracy and freedom,

I wish hereby to protest in this solemn forum. I do not feel it possible to associate myself with an ideological platform which has long since parted company with communism.

It is further to the writers' credit that the only adopted document that emerged from their ranks in this situation was the letter signed by a number of Slovak and Czech authors and read out by the poet Miroslav Válek.[16] It reflected the view of several of the Union's senior officials and other members who thought it needful to compromise with the Party centre and dissuade them, in the interests of the literary world, from extreme thoughts and actions. It was written very much *ad hoc* and it is hard to take it now at its face value. Some of those invited to sign it refused. It met the Party centre's wishes by criticising the proceedings of the Congress to date without passing the kind of judgement implied in the Lajčiak protest, and indeed it insisted on the legality and justification of all the discussions which had been objected to. As Jan Procházka put it to me later:

'It was intended to be our half of a bridge which we let down over the river, so that Jiří Hendrych could walk along it looking as if nothing had happened.'

If this gesture of goodwill was fated to be rejected, the signatories and those who sympathised with them could at least have a good conscience, in the knowledge that the decision to opt for repressive policies was purely of Hendrych's making. For even as Válek was reading out the letter, rumours were put around that the Party was about to instruct all communist writers to walk out. Since Party members were in the majority, this would mean the dissolution of the Congress; but it was also whispered that the end of the road had come for *Literární noviny*, for the *Litfond*, for the Union's publishing house and for the Union itself. I would not have given these stories any credence—but that I heard them the very next day uttered as a threat by Jiří Hendrych himself. What had happened meanwhile was that another speech had been made, this time by Ludvík Vaculík.

4
The plain truth about everything

Those who later described Vaculík's speech as a violent, unprecedented attack on the Party, the state, socialism, the working
class and everything else dear to them (though in such mouths
the words sound more alarming than endearing) had perhaps
read only a printed version of what he said. No doubt they would
have stuck to their opinion even if they had heard a tape record-
ing; but this, I think, is what one must hear to understand the
motives behind the words.

His delivery was calm and factual; he neither gestured nor
raised his voice for emphasis. Even the most dogged and rebellious passages, recalling the language and spirit of the manifestos
of the French Revolution, sounded in his delivery bitter and
nostalgic. Vaculík spoke with utter and surprising candour. He
made no use of subtle formulations or prudent innuendoes.
Listening to him, I realised how far we had accustomed ourselves
to wrap up all our criticisms and misgivings in a thick disguise so
that they should not only pass the censorship but also conform to
those standard patterns of public opinion which—we had come
to believe—must be accepted if there were to be any dialogue
without scandal and disgrace. Vaculík discarded these assump-
tions. His voice came loud and straight, but with no fanatical
pathos, no 'Shoot me if you will!' There was a contrast
and tension between his quiet manner and his emphatic
meaning that suggested a man disappointed to the hilt, a man
unwilling and unable to go on further, a man already driven
to the fringe of despair and determined to do—something,

but not something heroic. So he has no choice but to tell the truth.

When it was over I went out into the foyer and was nearly knocked over by an Ideological Department official, František Hubený, who was hurrying off somewhere. I had several times tried to persuade him that there was no truth in the 'stage-management' theory and that there was no *Literární noviny* clique conspiring to make anti-Party propaganda out of the Congress. Now he was bursting with indignation.

'What did I tell you? Do you still say there's no plot?'

In vain I tried to pacify him and explain that conspirators don't make speeches.

'If I were you I'd start worrying about your friends!'

It was in the afternoon session that Vaculík delivered his speech. When I had looked for him that morning someone told me he had been up all night writing it and was presumably still at work on the finishing touches. It must be clear to anyone who reads it that the speech had not come into being overnight; it was the fruit of long experience and meditation. Yet equally clearly it was a response to what had gone on at the Congress, to the claims and attitudes of the Party centre spokesmen which no longer offered hope of any useful dialogue or *modus vivendi* between rulers and writers. The core of Vaculík's speech was that the relationship between the Party leaders of the day and the creative community was a *relationship of power*, and that the course of the Congress had proved it despite all hopes to the contrary. It was this realisation that surely determined its tone, its sharp language and its treatment of the human situation of those 'men in power'. To address Hendrych personally by name as he did was a direct response to Hendrych's performance at the Party fraction meeting, and the passage would have been different if Hendrych had performed differently.

Vaculík turned up just before midday, ready to speak after the break. He complained that his trousers were too big round the waist and tried to find someone who could lend him a belt so that he shouldn't have to hold them up on the platform. But none of his friends had a belt to spare, and, since I had to drive from Vinohrady into the centre of Prague and back before the afternoon session, I took Vaculík with me so that we could hunt for a belt en route.

As we drove along we talked about the speech he was going to make. It was much on my mind that Vaculík was still on 'compulsory creative leave' from his post as an editor of *Literární noviny* and I was anxious that he should be able, as the outstanding journalist he was, to resume his work instead of having to stand on the sidelines.

'You've had plenty of trouble with the authorities,' I said. 'And you've got three children. So I hope there's nothing in your speech to cause a commotion.'

'No, funnily enough, there isn't,' he assured me.

'What are you going to say, then?'

'Oh, the same old things we've often talked about.' And he reminded me of the cook-and-chat sessions we had often enjoyed together.

I only mention this conversation as evidence that none of Vaculík's friends and colleagues had any idea what he was going to talk about. As conspirators we should certainly have been a wash-out. Just before it was his turn to go up to the platform, Vaculík passed his script to Ivan Klíma—we were all sitting at one table. Klíma looked through it quickly and ran off somewhere. When he came back he told me he had been frightened at the effect the speech might have in that atmosphere and felt the Party centre men might exploit it; so he had gone round to the platform to ask Jan Procházka if he didn't think it wiser to postpone this item till later.

'It's very strong stuff,' he had told him, 'and they'll say we've been organising things again.'

Procházka, as ignorant of the text as everybody except Klíma and the author, reacted typically.

'Nobody's organising anything here. There's only one rule in force and that's for everybody to say what he wants. If somebody doesn't like it that's not our fault.'

Klíma heartily agreed. And this consultation was the sum total of 'stage-management' behind Vaculík's speech, which he proceeded to deliver when his turn came according to the order in which names had been submitted.

It was a fine warm evening and Sergěj Machonín, Alexander Kliment and I sat outside on the terrace of a little wine restaurant near the Loreta. We were worried about Vaculík. With no obvious connection Machonín started to tell us about incidents he remembered from his concentration-camp days in the last war; incidents involving people in extreme situations. Unlike many others he had never talked to us about them before; but this evening he described the whole range of behaviour men and women are capable of when there is nothing else left—from brutality to marvellous valour.

It crossed our minds that in his novel *The Axe*, which had just recently been published, Vaculík deals with something of this sort. His hero deliberately creates a situation where he is cut off from any chance of escape and has to do what he had resolved but feared he lacked the courage for.

Vaculík had really said no more this afternoon than he had already written in *The Axe*, it seemed to us; perhaps a little less. It was all there. But on publication the book had created nothing like the sensation it made after the speech. Until then it could be bought in any shop; it was quickly sold out when the word went round that its author had spoken at the Writers' Congress and *how* he had spoken. Originally some of the critics had found a fault or two; the *Rudé právo* reviewer had complained that it was politically vague. But no one had seen it as an attack on socialism. There was a run on the book in the Party's Central Committee library—but only after Vaculík's speech had been cyclostyled and distributed as a confidential document for consideration by the Presidium. (These were the first copies made; many others were to circulate throughout the country later.) Here was another example of the distorted vision that prevailed in our public life: what was permissible in a novel, since it could be interpreted as metaphorical, provoked a scandal when it was put in the direct language of a public speech.

But what, in fact, had Vaculík really said?

To be sure, he had criticised the Party centre of the time, the 'ruling circles' as he called them, in a way which shocked almost everyone. But were his criticisms unjust? The impact they made was mainly due to the way in which he had declared openly what most people had known or felt for a long time. As he said right at the beginning of his speech: 'I am using this opportunity to tell you what you already know without my help'—and there was no false modesty in this. Was it that his language was so drastic? Other governments are constantly criticised, and far more savagely. A little while ago on the West German television I heard an anti-government harangue by the Catholic writer Heinrich Böll. He maintained that the government in power was unfit to lead the nation in political affairs and demanded that it should limit itself to purely administrative functions. Piling on the insults, Böll added that he would then judge the authorities by their ability to keep the dustbins emptied regularly. Nothing happened to him beyond the Federal Chancellor treating him with the same sarcasm and calling him a 'yapping terrier'.

In a normal society unjust criticism is met with counter-arguments and evidence, and if the party criticised is a government it will have better means of presenting its case than the individual critic. But it would have been naive in Czechoslovakia to point out the normal state of affairs. Vaculík's speech shocked society precisely because it transcended the accepted limits and showed no respect for the conventions that ruled our lives. Many of us had succumbed so far that we questioned the utility of the stand he made and reproached him for bringing to a head the conflict that had festered for so many years. If this was a normal reaction, it was normal only by the standards of that total abnormality which surrounded us.

As we sat there it was Vaculík himself who occupied our minds above all. I expected him to be arrested. Not overtly because of his speech (though that would be the real reason) but on some other charge: it was always possible to find an excuse if you tried hard enough. Even if he remained at liberty he would not have an easy time. He would be out of a job, and his wife too—except for the kind of jobs considered suitable in such cases. Their children would be given a hard time in school and it would shortly transpire that they 'lacked talent' to justify further study. His book would be stopped, his articles would not be published and he would find it impossible to make ends meet. They would have to live even more frugally than now, perhaps in real poverty.

Alexander Kliment, though he wished Vaculík no ill, took a different view. He must have foreseen all these possibilities, he said, and if he nevertheless acted as he had done, he must have felt the need to. He must surely, then, feel easier in himself than before.

With these thoughts we went on our ways. I got home to find a telegram from the Party's Central Committee summoning all the communist writers to a fraction meeting at nine the following morning. The Congress itself was deferred until this meeting had finished.

Although all the Party members received this message in good time many of the non-communist writers naturally failed to learn of the postponement. When we turned up for the nine o'clock meeting, therefore, we found many of our colleagues standing around and obliged to wait outside till our private deliberations were over. The usual embarrassing situation, familiar from the Union's central committee sessions, was thus repeated on a larger scale.

Surrounded by an entourage of functionaries, Jiří Hendrych was now seen to re-enter the hall for the first time since he left it during the reading of the Solzhenitsyn letter. One of the officials was a man I had known since he had helped me, over the censor's opposition, to get access to archives I needed for a study of the Heydrich assassination. An historian by training, he had now become one of Hendrych's unofficial advisors.

'Is it going to be bad?' I asked him.

He was taken aback. We had not seen each other for a long time and he evidently failed for a moment to place me, though he certainly knew I was due to take over the Writers' Union weekly.

'Not bad: just tough,' was his answer. 'It will depend on you . . .'

He seemed sorry that his position obliged him to adopt these delphic formulae and, hoping to strike a more friendly note, he switched to the subject that interested him most at the moment, if only out of curiosity.

'I say, which of the people here is Vaculík?'

I had just left Ludvík standing with a knot of friends a few yards away, so I pointed him out.

'I'll introduce you if you like . . .'

'No, no. No need for that.' He took me off nervously in the

opposite direction. Evidently things *were* going to be bad, as well as tough.

'We've had a job with him,' the historian went on. 'Spent the whole night drawing up reports for the boss, searching right through Bakunin, Johann Marx . . .'

'Are you trying to make Vaculík into an anarchist?'

'Couldn't find a thing.' The frustration of the night's work still showed in his voice. 'Good God, where does that Vaculík man get it all from?'

I told him his department could have saved themselves the trouble. Vaculík had certainly never read any of the anarchist classics and if they wanted to find out what lay behind his speech to the Congress they ought to look around at everyday life instead of in libraries.

He hesitated and was going to ask me another question when the chairman started to open the fraction meeting. In the chair this time was Vasil Bil'ak, then secretary for ideological affairs in the Central Committee of the Slovak Communist Party. He expressed 'serious dissatisfaction' at the course of the Congress and announced that certain measures would be necessary. These measures were so urgent, he said, that they could not be debated at all by the present meeting but must simply be passed by vote. The Congress was due to resume at ten, in an hour's time. Bil'ak then gave the floor to Jiří Hendrych to state the position of the delegates of the Czechoslovak Central Committee.

Hendrych plunged straight in. It was clear from what had happened at the Congress so far, and especially from some of the individual speeches, that we were dealing with a group acting in concert, and with opinions contrary to the Party line. As a result, a psychosis had been expertly generated that was hostile to state, Party and national interests. The attempts to misuse the Congress for these purposes had culminated in the openly anti-state and anti-Party presentation of the writer Vaculík. (The substitution of 'writer' for 'comrade' was a conventional Party gimmick, as much as to say: 'Vaculík is now outside the Party in my eyes, even if he is sitting right in front of me'.)

There was no time for a detailed analysis, Hendrych went on, of who else had acted against the Party and on what occasions. Briefly, the Party condemned all attempts to blacken the past efforts of our people and to speak of them as a 'Dark Age' or to make comparisons with the Nazi occupation. He paused for a moment to consider the sins of another delegate, Pavel Kohout, before returning to the first target. What were Vaculík and people like him aiming at? What did Havel and *his* sort want? 'Vaculík, what *do* you want?' He recalled 1956 in Hungary. That had started in the same way, and ended with open fighting. But there was a limit to patience. 'We shall not leave matches in the hands of irresponsible elements and anarchists!' Vaculík had parted company with communism; he had attacked the Party in a way unprecedented since February 1948. And Hendrych uttered what in a normal society would not have been a threat at all, but in ours sounded like a call to war. 'Suppose we transfer the debate elsewhere, to the whole Party. How would it look if we published Vaculík's speech in the Party press?'

The worst thing is that we were all able to imagine only too vividly just what a 'Party discussion' would be like, with all the *pros* silenced beforehand and only the indignant *cons* allowed to raise their voices. No one would be able to tell which voices stood for something genuine—either sincerely felt opinions or views warped by official propaganda—and which merely demonstrated the smooth functioning of the Party machine, long since equipped to manufacture *vox populi* in any quantities and styling that the Centre required. How often we had heard those spontaneously applauded resolutions, those outbursts of righteous anger pouring in unanimously from all corners of the country! How we had marvelled at the identity of opinions sent in from 'Škoda Works employees, Plzeň', or 'collective farm workers, Michalovce', from 'schoolteachers of the Přerov district' and 'North Bohemian textile firms' . . . Obviously what Hendrych was threatening would be no debate at all, but a campaign whose true background would be almost unknown even to those attacked, but whose outcome would be known to its organisers from the start.

Later, in 1968, when Vaculík's speech was published without any accompanying pogrom, there was no commotion at all and everyone who read it thought whatever they wished to think. But at the time of which we are speaking Hendrych's promise of a Party-wide 'discussion' was a threat effective enough, he knew, to try and extort concessions with.

'The proceedings of the Congress so far make it imperative to draw certain conclusions about the list of candidates for, and the composition of, the next central committee of the Writers' Union.'

We had already seen, in fact, that the 'conclusions' in question had been drawn before the Congress had had any proceedings. The only difficulty had been that the first meeting of the Party fraction had failed to accept those conclusions. At this second meeting, however, their acceptance was judged both possible and necessary. Hendrych accordingly went on in the tone of one simply delivering instructions without any attempt to justify what he was saying:

'The Central Committee of the Czechoslovak Communist Party binds all Party members to vote in favour of the new list of candidates both in the electoral commission and in the full session of the Congress. If this should fail, they will leave the Congress and refuse to accept any responsibility for its consequences. That of course will mean the end of the Union,' he concluded. I vividly remember his gesture: the two outstretched arms and the thumbs down.

Before the head of the Ideological Department could even read out the new list of candidates for the Union's committee as drawn up by the Party's Secretariat, a woman writer, Hela Volanská, asked to speak. She did so with such vigour that Bil'ak felt unable to refuse, even though it had been decided to allow no discussion. Evidently she had been seriously alarmed by the prospect of an anti-intellectual campaign, which Hendrych's threats implied; once on her feet, she launched into a sincerely passionate defence of all the people under fire and tried to argue the spokesmen of the Party leadership out of taking extreme measures. Bil'ak's answer to this was simply that he had no choice once the fundamental principles of the state had been questioned. However, since he had allowed Volanská to speak he could not refuse the floor to Vaculík. Two sentences summed up what *he* now had to say.

'I spoke because I wanted for once to have things straightened out in myself. I challenged myself to say the plain truth about everything, because the plain truth is something I hardly ever find myself telling these days.'

When I heard this I could not help thinking of the previous night's talk with Kliment and Machonín. Kliment had been right when he said Vaculík would be feeling better now, despite all the danger.

One could see Vaculík steeling himself to keep his voice steady as he confessed that, sincerely as he had meant every word, he had been afraid the day before and was afraid again now. He had, of course, no political aspirations. 'No one with any ambition talks the way I do. I have suggested nothing illegal; I have only called for reform.' He rejected, then, the description of his speech as anti-state or anti-Party and asked Hendrych to tell him if he still stood by those words.

Hendrych was obviously in no mood for argument and Havlíček prepared himself to read out the new list of candidates. But Vaculík, from the body of the hall, again demanded an answer from Hendrych. Klíma and I were sitting at the same table as Vaculík and we could see how deeply concerned he was. 'I only wish you could go through what I have gone through!' It sounded impudent, but really it was a gesture toward Hendrych that only Vaculík would have made, challenging him naively but without malice to put aside the role of second-most-powerful-man-in-the-country and speak out simply as a plain, honest man. Perhaps it was the last time Hendrych ever had the chance.

Nothing, however, was further from the Secretary's thoughts. He was there to represent the Party centre, the man of power representing the body that wielded power over him. If he could not play the plain, honest man, at least he honestly reflected the nature of that power. He spoke abruptly and without notes now; his style was disjointed and crude.

'What sort of authority are you to talk about the nation? and the parliamentary deputies? and the schoolteachers?' he threw back at Vaculík, the bit about the schoolteachers (whom Vaculík had not mentioned) being a subconscious reference, perhaps, to the profession he had once belonged to himself. 'Your speech was all anarchism—with a good deal of arrogance thrown in! It sounds ridiculous, but what you're really asking is for the working class to have its power taken away: that's what you really mean, underneath all your talk about "civilising the authorities . . ."'

Vaculík could stand it no longer. He took a deep breath and shouted: 'That isn't true!' And again, after the next insinuation: 'That isn't either!'

It may seem absurd, but what rose out of the depths of my memory at that moment was a vivid picture of Klement Gottwald making his maiden speech in a tumultuous parliament, back in 1929, flinging bitter accusations into the faces of those fellow-deputies who then represented the powers-that-be. We had re-read his address many a time in school. But the Communist Party has long since lost the glamour of standing in justified opposition against authority; now it is itself the ruling power and here was its mouthpiece at work.

I was aroused from this reverie by hearing Klíma trying to interrupt Vaculík. 'Stop! Don't be a fool!'

'What do you expect me to say, then?'

'Shut up!' Klíma and I shouted at him together.

He turned his back on us and fell bitterly silent.

Hendrych too, oddly enough, seemed embarrassed by this scene, mumbled something and hurried on to an awkward conclusion.

At this point Havlíček thought fit to bring out his list of candidates again. Out of the thirty names approved at the first Party fraction meeting, eleven had now been removed on orders from the *apparat* and replaced by others. Those to be dropped were Jiří Brabec, Čivrný, Havel, Jungmann, Klíma, Kohout, Karel Kosík, Šotola, Jan Trefulka, Vaculík and František Vrba—obviously those whom the Party centre regarded as belonging to the '*Literární noviny* group' or being somehow associated with it by their criticisms of official policy.

Most of those present were staggered by this proposal, but Bil'ak was still eager to have it voted on forthwith as a 'democratically approved resolution'. In addition to his previous threats he now pleaded shortage of time and showed touching concern for the non-communist delegates who were having to wait outside for so long.

Eduard Goldstücker, however, now rose to say that no Writers' Union committee formed in this way could be considered representative and, since he could not sit in such a committee himself, he asked that his own name should be removed from the list. This was a grave step to take, but refusal to participate was by then the only way left to express disagreement. Equally impressive was the identity of the man who chose to act in this way, for Goldstücker was a pre-war communist who had shown his loyalty to the Party in the most difficult times, had always been notably moderate and had gone out of his way at this Congress, as we saw, to find compromise agreements on the 'rules of the game'. The gesture, even if it was not understood by all the Party centre men present, certainly went home with Hendrych, who realised that he had gone too far. And when Kundera, Jan Skácel, Jindřiška Smetanová, František Pavlíček and others all proceeded to renounce their candidatures too, and more candidates then asked to speak with the obvious intention of doing likewise, Hendrych found his whole policy in ruins. For there was now a real danger that the Congress would break up as a result of his intervention, which was supported by only a few of the less prominent delegates.

Hendrych accordingly took over and withdrew Havlíček's proposal. Instead, he proposed that the list should remain as it had been approved by the first meeting of the Union's communist members, save only for the candidature of those who had made anti-Party speeches at the Congress, namely Vaculík, Klíma, Havel and Kohout. These should be replaced, he suggested, by Ivan Skála, Josef Hanzlík, Oldřich Šuleř and Norbert Frýd. This compromise was a good deal more acceptable than the first proposal and, whether it was a prearranged tactic or a piece of improvisation by Hendrych, it was undoubtedly a skilful move.

How our vision is blurred by the scuffles and bargains of the political game, blinding us to the real course of events and the real balance of power! The agreement we had been forced to make seemed to many of us not merely passable, but in some ways a positive victory, and received a clear majority of votes both at the fraction meeting and in the full Congress subsequently. J. R. Pick's counter-proposal that Skála, Hanzlík, Šuleř and Frýd be struck off the list and Vaculík, Klíma, Havel and Kohout restored was regarded as a mere gesture of defiance and rejected by the Congress.

So the Fourth Congress of Czechoslovak Writers ended—inevitably, in our country—in compromise. It was a compromise taken as a whole, and a compromise for the various groups and interests within the Union. Only the future can tell for whom the compromise was honourable and useful, or whether indeed the whole thing was not a pointless revolt that did more harm than good.

The general character and outcome of the Congress were of course warped by the Party apparatus with its continual interferences and interpretations. The writers were given no chance to concentrate on discussing the role of literature in the nation's development against its European background. The debate soon deviated from the *Draft Programme* prepared by the Union's own committee and presented by Kundera with his own added comment. The irritation with which the authorities reacted to these texts showed that they felt threatened by the mere fact of discussion at such a serious level, for this in itself tended to expose the essential poverty of the stalinist version of socialism. This system was not merely distasteful to the creators of literature but even more repugnant to the rest of society. And it seemed logical to those in command that if they allowed destructive, or even analytical, criticism at one point this would endanger the whole web at whose centre they stood, fixed in their own rigid notions and propped up by the machinery of their own power. Anyone who dwelt on this theme in open discussion and referred to it in these terms was pursued with increasing suspicion and vindictiveness. Hendrych offered the Congress every encouragement to discuss the role of literature in the narrow and outmoded context of stalinist socialism; but most of the writers, in the light of their own experiences, literary and otherwise, regarded this offer as both immoral and a waste of time.

Since this fundamental disagreement could not be openly discussed—the Party centre had a thousand ways of preventing that —it is not surprising that an outlet was found in all sorts of quarrels over issues whose solution should have been self-evident. Moreover, in the course of its own stage-management the Party apparatus introduced all kinds of fictitious popular demands (like the 'demand' for the silencing of *Literární noviny* and the critical thinking that went with it) and impossible proposals (such as the suppression of that paper by 'healthy elements' in the literary community itself).

Only a profound ignorance of how things stood in the Czecho-slovak literary world and in society generally could have fathered the notion that it was only necessary to isolate, and then crush, a tiny group of malevolent men around one newspaper to gain the support of most creative writers for the official cultural line. Such fantasies were the result of that gradual degeneration of Party work over the years, by which the *apparat* had abandoned any serious attempt to establish facts in favour of predetermined dogmas spawned from the brains of a small circle of men and indeed, often enough, solely from the brain of Comrade Number One, whose decisions had to be both obeyed and justified by everyone else. This was the state of affairs that led many of the more intelligent and competent men higher in the Party (as else-where in society) to resign from such work when they found that they were expected to support policies calculated to turn every chronic crisis into an acute one. Those who succeeded them and tried, often sincerely enough, to carry out these instructions ended by becoming both victims and executors of projects which reflected nothing but the lowering of Party standards. Function-aries selected and conditioned in this way had then to rely on information from others of the same stamp, so that they only heard what they wanted to hear, or what the Party centre thought they should hear. In the literary world things went so far that official credence was given only to the complaints of men who had themselves failed to win recognition, and petty tales from informants or even known alcoholics were taken as the best guide to reality. Having failed to establish its own hegemony inside the Writers' Union, the Party centre listened only to ambitious and malcontent voices at ground level. It could have gleaned far more useful evidence from the many outstanding individuals and groups who had been victimised in earlier purges and were no longer even active authors.

Reliance on worthless sources of information meant that increasingly 'solutions' were adopted that bore no relation to the needs they were supposed to satisfy, and when they were im-plemented gave rise to one crisis after another. Artificially induced though such crises were, they naturally intensified the mistrust and animosity of men in the Party centre, who began to see everywhere 'opposition forces', 'anti-Party trends', 'left and right deviations' and, finally, 'enemies', however hard those 'enemies' protested that they were no such thing. And if they did not give up at the first blow, that showed only what cunning enemies they were—practically proof positive that conspiracy was afoot.

Whenever, in politics, distinct and even opposed streams of thought are lumped together as one large conspiracy, it is a sure symptom of a supreme crisis in the policy pursued. For when a system abandons political methods in favour of detective methods, known as 'state security' operations, it negates itself and writes its own death-warrant.

Given the hierarchical structure of power as it was in Czechoslovakia, however, who had the chance to be well informed, to discern true causes, make correct analyses and offer sensible solutions to problems? Anyone who supplied accurate information would be suspected of some crime or other and be replaced by a different informer; anyone who put his finger on the real culprits would be accused of defamation; anyone who proposed practicable solutions to problems would be labelled hostile, identified with 'the opposition platform' and made into an 'anti-socialist' even if it was only the official version of socialism he objected to. But then, officially, there was no other.

Just as the events surrounding the Fourth Writers' Congress seemed to reflect in miniature the whole state of our society, so the crisis of the Party centre on that occasion reflected the larger crisis of the whole stalinist system; the local conflict anticipated the wider one, the attempt at a solution foreshadowed both the hopes and fears of the next attempt, with all its honest endeavours and its wretched limitations. It was only because of these clearly-felt analogies that our Congress meant any more to the Czechoslovak public than other such occasions had done.

To the Party leaders the Fourth Congress only meant a very partial victory: they had foiled the election of four men to the Union's committee. And even that had cost them great effort and it had been apparent that the decision was an imposed one. However, what could not be achieved by one method today they would surely achieve by other methods tomorrow. It was to this end that the Party and state authorities now bent their efforts.

5
Inside the ideology department

The trouble started right after the Congress. It was proposed as an obvious journalistic duty to include in the next number of *Literární noviny* the text of the final resolution, which had after all been passed unanimously. However, the censors refused to let the full text be published, demanding the omission of the following sentence:

> Disapproving as it does of the present practice of press surveillance, the Fourth Congress instructs the central committee of the Czechoslovak Writers' Union to take the initiative in assessing the results of this practice during the initial period of validity of the Press Law with a view to limiting censorship to national defence matters.

It is ironical that the first bone of contention with the censor's office after the Writers' Congress should have been the censorship itself. The executives of the 'Central Publishing Board' were asking, in fact, for the excision of passages concerning their own institution; otherwise, they assured us, they had no objection to a single word.

Those who had pleaded at the Congress for a radical reform of the censorship were not literary cranks but men reacting to plain facts. The censor had already made the appearance of many books and films difficult or impossible; his ravages were still more oppressive in the fields of radio, television and the press, and most of all in the case of *Literární noviny*. Every week's issue involved procedures of immense complexity. If this sort of thing were to continue the paper's days would soon be numbered. The Congress had wished to point out how intolerable the present state of affairs was, to try and alleviate it for the moment and to find a way leading to a more permanent solution. Instead of which the censor was now trying to veto the Congress's very conclusions on the subject!

The Central Publishing Board had in the past concerned itself with films, books and articles—products of individual effort, whose authors could negotiate with the censor and then either reach an agreement with him or simply take note of his decisions and comply with them. But the present case concerned a resolution collectively approved by the writers who constituted their Union's central committee. For these writers to have collective dealings with the censor would have required another session of their Congress; but the Congress had dispersed several days back. In any case the Congress had already discussed censorship and summarised its thoughts very pointedly in its final resolution, the one now at issue. Could anyone think that its view now would differ from that of a few days ago?

Clearly, however, the Party centre's obstructions were not to be interpreted in terms of previous practice. They were simply a challenge flung in the face of the literary community, and the only possible reply was to say that if the resolution was not to be printed intact it would not be printed at all. *Literární noviny* would not be acting responsibly towards its readers if it agreed to issue a mutilated version of the Congress resolution as if it were the whole text, without being able even to hint that anything had been cut. The Congress was over, the public had scarcely been told a word about it, the next issue of the paper was eagerly awaited. Was it to appear without any reference to the Congress and devote its front-page story to the beauties of summer?

This argument carried the day. No final decisions had yet been reached in the Party centre (which was also the censor's headquarters) on how to react to the Congress either internally or publicly; documents were still being studied and memoranda drawn up. And so Juraj Špitzer, as he sighed with relief at the end of his period of office as First Secretary of the Writers' Union and packed his bags before returning home to Bratislava, was able to undertake one more task. When he was told of the censor's decision about the resolution and of the logical consequence that it could not be published at all, he put through a call to Jiří Hendrych. Pointing out the implications of the censor's move he recalled an agreement the two of them had reached during the Congress, namely that material reflecting both opposing viewpoints should be published in parallel, both in *Literární noviny* and in the Slovak writers' weekly *Kultúrny život*. Hendrych reluctantly acknowledged that he had come to such an agreement and agreed to the publication of the Congress resolution as it had been passed, without change or deletion.

The censorship officials, when told of this, refused to believe it and several hours passed before they could be satisfied. I hate to imagine the remarks that must have been exchanged on the internal Party telephone network. However, they gave way in the end and the censor's stamp duly appeared on the licensing proof of *Literární noviny*.

So it came about that, for the first time in all those years, the Czechoslovak reader was formally acquainted with the existence of press censorship through a single sentence in the Congress resolution. This was an important moment. From then on censorship had to be justified and defended, and the most skilful defence of censorship is an embarrassment to the authorities, who thereby admit that their tenure of power requires it. Very soon we were to see the censor's office taking the initiative to put an end to the period of uncertainty and urging their superiors to make a firm stand: they clearly regarded the publication of the resolution *in toto* as a piece of prevarication.

Up to this time we had imagined that both the writers' papers would reprint the Congress debate in its entirety as they had on previous occasions, even when things had also run far from smoothly. The ban on reproducing the debate in the *daily* press would apply, we assumed, only to them; for the literary journals we expected the only problem would be how to comment on the speeches. To publish what had been said at the Union's meeting appeared to us in any case the obvious duty of the Union's own organ and no one had assumed that any obstacle would be put in the way of fulfilling this duty. Accordingly we sent all the Congress documents and speeches to be printed, and distributed proofs to those concerned so that they could check the accuracy of the stenographers' record against their original scripts. The authors had already sent these back to us and we were all set to publish the entire transcript of the Congress proceedings in the next two numbers of *Literární noviny*, which were to be four pages larger than normal.

Before we could go to press, however, we were bidden to a meeting at which there would be representatives of the Ideological Department of the Party's Central Committee, of the Central Publishing Board and of the Writers' Union as well as people from our own editorial office. At this meeting the Ideological Department's spokesman, Josef Hotmar, informed us that the Party's Central Committee had decided to start political disciplinary proceedings against Klíma, Kohout, Liehm and Vaculík, whose speeches (he said) had been directed against the Party and therefore must not be published, certainly not before the proceedings were concluded. For the same reasons publication of Havel's speech was also forbidden even though he was not a member of the Communist Party and no Party action could be instituted against him. Publication of the speeches by Kliment and Jan Skácel was vetoed pending further notice. (Kliment's speech was released, however, in the course of the meeting on the understanding that his conclusions and proposals would be left out, and Skácel's was also released after a telephone conversation with the Party's Regional Committee in Brno. For the text of his speech had been previously banned from publication in the Brno journal *Host do domu* but the Regional Committee now withdrew its ban.) A temporary ban was also placed on Novomeský's speech until the Slovak Communist Party authorities had discussed it with him. (When they did, it was suggested that he leave out the whole passage on censorship and only publish the final section on Czech-Slovak relations, about a quarter of the whole. Since this part derived its whole weight and meaning from the preceding critique of censorship Novomeský refused, and his speech remained prohibited.) Partial objections were also raised at this meeting to the speeches by Kundera, Goldstücker, Hamšík, Hanzlík and Petr Kabeš, which could be printed only if amendments were agreed between the *Literární noviny* editors and the Central Publishing Board. (These 'partial' objections turned out to be so radical that the authors, for the most part, refused to accept the proposed cuts and changes as distorting their views and falsifying the whole object of their case.) The remaining speeches could be passed, we were told, provided we removed all anti-Party and anti-state remarks. The term 'anti-state', as we found out from the list of proposed amendments to Goldstücker's speech and as was then openly admitted by our interlocuters, covered *inter alia* any critical reference to the censor's activities.

Clearly, not much of the Congress record would have been left if we had accepted all these requirements; it was essential to make a firm stand and demand that they be modified. However, it was not clear how to do this at a time when the Union was virtually leaderless. For Jan Procházka, the chairman-designate of the Union's new committee, had been told by Hendrych in the course of the Congress that the Party Presidium had ruled against his accepting the post until the conclusion of a Party enquiry—which had not even begun—into his attitude on the Arab-Israeli conflict and into the Congress generally. Šotola and Špitzer had ended their terms of office as secretary and chairman of the outgoing committee simultaneously with the end of the Congress. And when a brief session of the committee had been held immediately afterwards to elect a small steering presidium this had been vetoed by officials of the Party *apparat* on the grounds that the composition of such a presidium had first to be cleared in one of the Party's top bodies. So the Writers' Union had neither a chairman nor a presidium; all it had was a forty-five-member central committee which was not allowed to convene until the Party's own Central Committee had prepared and called a separate meeting of its communist members. No one could say when this might occur, not even the spokesmen of the Party centre, who were still trying to get clear in their own minds what they were going to be able to do in practice with the literary community. One way and another, then, the Union had been completely paralysed and was leading an almost illegal existence.

The only properly elected organ of the Union which was at the moment allowed to hold meetings without the prior consent of the Party *apparat* was in fact the editorial board of *Literární noviny*. In all the tension of the preceding months its members had established the habit of regular fortnightly gatherings. All those who were in Prague and not too preoccupied with other matters would come along every other Monday afternoon to join in a discussion from which, alas, literary topics were increasingly displaced by arguments about the latest rulings and interventions of the Party Secretariat and the censor's office.

Even before telling the editorial board about the latest demands of the Ideological Department and censorship officials I rang up Juraj Špitzer, now my opposite number—for he had taken up his new post as editor-in-chief of *Kultúrny život* in Bratislava. We agreed that our two papers should apply the same principles in publishing their records of the Writers' Congress, keeping in step throughout. I sent the authorised texts of the speeches to Bratislava and agreed with Špitzer which speech should appear in what issue—all labour in vain, as it turned out. I remember my temperamental colleague's curses ringing out when I told him what restrictions the authorities wanted to impose. If a tape-recording of this conversation has been kept anywhere it will provide evidence of Špitzer's sincere indignation, not always expressed in very literary Slovak. More important, however, he told me exactly what had been agreed between himself and Hendrych during the Congress about the subsequent reprinting of speeches in the writers' journals. Hendrych's consent at that time to publication in the form of a 'confrontation' between all views on both sides, *pro* and *con*, had now been flagrantly contradicted.

For *Literární noviny* there was a special significance in what Špitzer was telling me, since at the time when he came to this agreement with Hendrych he had still been First Secretary of the Union. His account of it was thus the only evidence of the position of the Union's officials which our paper could invoke at a time when their successors were prevented from meeting or even from being chosen.

I told Špitzer the editorial board would have another meeting to talk about ways and means of publishing the Congress records in view of the latest prohibitions, and I was confident there would be another encounter with the censors and Party officials. Špitzer then asked me to represent him at this encounter and quote his conversation with Hendrych. I was to say that he, Špitzer, insisted on the agreement being upheld; that even if for some obscure reason the Kohout speech had to be suppressed there were still no grounds for withholding an abridged version of Vaculík's; that nothing beyond appropriate editing ought to be done to Havel's, Klíma's, Liehm's and other contributions that had been queried; and that if this view were rejected it would be better to print nothing at all, for the editors' responsibility to the committee of the Union and to the writers in general would not allow them to present a radically distorted impression of the Congress.

Such were Špitzer's feelings about the maximum length to which we could go in complying with the Party centre's demands, if it was to be worth while reprinting anything from the Congress at all. The editorial board of *Literární noviny* were prepared to go further, so that the public could gather at least the main lines of the Congress debate. The ideal thing would of course be to reproduce everything, unamended, and the board seriously considered whether it would not, after all, be better to insist on this line and otherwise print nothing. But after long discussion it agreed to meet the Party centre half-way and make concessions so as to enable some of the speeches to be published in part, rather than consign all that intellectual effort to limbo. It was realised that the correctness of the compromise was disputable; the members of the board were not happy in reaching this agreement, but they decided in the end to accept the risk of being attacked over it. They passed a resolution, then, in the form of a letter to Jiří Hendrych and to František Havlíček as head of the Central Committee's Ideological Department. 'The editorial board', it ran,

1. accepts the exclusion of speeches made in the debate by comrades Kohout and Vaculík, which were described as 'anti-Party' in an official statement by the leader of the Party delegation, comrade Hendrych;
2. rejects the description of the speeches by comrades Klíma, Liehm and Havel as 'anti-Party' and takes the view that these should be printed after abridgement and editing along the same lines as other speeches;*

* The editors had agreed with the authors on the omission of passages meaningful only in the full context of the Congress itself. In compliance

3. considers it essential to publish the entire speech of comrade Kundera, since this was the point of departure for the whole proceedings of the Congress and a number of other contributors were directly or indirectly responding to it;

4. in view of comrade Novomeský's moral standing and authority in questions of cultural policy, considers it essential to publish his speech; and with a view to expediting publication of the Congress records agrees in this case to a week's delay to enable the relevant authorities to discuss their representations with comrade Novomeský, even though this involves departing from the chronological order of publication;

5. accepts the recommendations of the Central Publishing Board for changes to be made in the speeches of comrades Hanzlík and Hamšík, but does not agree to the recommended cuts in those by comrades Goldstücker and Kabeš;

6. has authorised comrades Procházka, Kundera and Hamšík to negotiate this resolution with the competent representatives of the Central Committee of the Czechoslovak Communist Party.

The reader might conclude from the text of this letter that the running of a newspaper in those days required the diplomat's skills more than any other qualifications. I admit that I favoured the path of diplomacy and compromise at that time, though it was far from natural to me. I had no particular experience in that line, but it seemed clear to me that if nothing at all, in the end, appeared about the Congress on the pages of *Literární noviny* it would be the paper's editors who would be blamed for it. And since there would be no possibility at all for us to defend our stance *coram publico*, and even in the literary world only through private conversation, a certain amount of odium would inevitably remain with us. *Etwas bleibt immer hängen.* I therefore asked the board to grant something like plenipotentiary powers to the three of us

with the Congress's own resolution all references to the Solzhenitsyn letter were also left out. These principles—implied by Špitzer in such phrases as 'an abridged version of Vaculík' and 'appropriate editing' of others—were accepted by all the authors, who authorised their texts for publication in *Literární noviny* accordingly.

who had been given the job of dealing with those 'competent representatives' of the Party's Central Committee, and so we were empowered to negotiate different terms than the ones outlined in the board's letter if they seemed acceptable and feasible to us.

Hendrych, inevitably, was too busy with other urgent jobs to receive us and we dealt only with the second addressee of the letter, František Havlíček. Our meeting, one of the most curious experiences of my life, is engraved on my memory as a symbol of the grotesquely abnormal conditions in which we lived. Not that countless other episodes from that period were not equally sensational or dramatic. But few can have been so replete with unintended comedy as this interview which, with its preparation, occupied us all for a complete afternoon without yielding any result whatsoever.

It was an odd assortment of men who came together that day in the austerely furnished office of the head of the Ideological Department. Behind the desk where we had seen, in their days, the flexible and quick-witted Pavel Auersperg,[17] the mournful, good-hearted Jaroslav Hes and many others of his predecessors, there now sat a weary, absent-minded man, with the air of a tolerant uncle to whom the whole business was repugnant and regrettable. He had hardly had time to eat lunch, Havlíček complained, and he still had to write a speech for that evening. 'I expect you're hoping to kill me with worry,' he told us reproachfully as he shook our hands.

Jan Procházka, robust and energetic, took a seat at his right hand: a man incensed by the whole recent behaviour of the Party centre and convinced that its leaders, having brought it to the brink of an abyss, were about to send it hurtling into the depths. He minced no words and was forever itching to pound the table with his fist; only today the terms of his mission made him—reluctantly—milder.

A little way off, as if to indicate his distaste for any dealings with such suspect partners, sat a pallid plain-clothes officer, Colonel E. Kovařík, head of the Central Publications Board. He took no part in the discussion except to follow it in the sense of browsing continuously through a large file of censored texts stamped Top Secret, so that he always had some incriminating quotation at his fingertips to upset our arguments with. He abandoned his gloomy silence only when he saw Havlíček giving way to us on any point; then he would say that he had no option but to appeal to the 'executive' responsible to the government for the work of his Board, namely to the Minister of the Interior. He sounded as he said it like a police sergeant about to arrest us for a breach of the peace.

Milan Kundera, by contrast, sat amongst us like a man from another world. When asked to comment on a specific point he would bridle visibly; one could see the contempt welling up in him for the crude presumptions of our antagonists. Kundera had for a long time resisted all our attempts to bring him into this meeting. He had made it clear that he felt utter loathing for anyone whose job was to censor and prohibit other people's work, that he was neither anxious nor able to sit down with a man who could even contemplate the task of classifying thoughts into legal and illegal categories. Only the fact that we were committed to urging publication of his entire speech, by which he set great store, induced him to cross the threshold into an office he had never wanted to see and whose very existence struck him as the height of irrelevance. It was no easy task, again, to persuade a man like Kundera that some minor concessions might be needed if we were to issue a text that did him any sort of justice. He agreed reluctantly—perhaps only because the appearance in print of some of his other articles would depend on the outcome of the present negotiations.

Havlíček started off with a lengthy explanation of the Presidium's decision to order Party proceedings against Klíma, Kohout, Liehm and Vaculík. His tone was not aggressive but almost nostalgic, as if he were sorry that things had come to such a pass and made his own position that much more difficult. He interspersed his lectures with quotations from a speech Novotný had just made at the Party High School, attacking the Writers' Congress and proclaiming a tough line along the whole 'ideological front'. An extract from this statement, which (as we later discovered) orthodox officials were already trying to use as the basis for a campaign to bolshevise the whole country's literary scene with the help of army commissars, had appeared that very day in *Rudé právo*. What Havlíček was reading from, however, was a cyclostyled version and he pointed out, wagging his finger at us, that we were hearing unpublished passages intended for internal Party use and not for the public. He behaved, in fact, like a schoolmaster hoping to impress a group of truants with extracts from the confidential minutes of a staff meeting and hinting that, while others might take a grimmer view of their misdeeds, he himself was inclined to be tolerant and give them a fair chance.

Whenever we opposed our own arguments to his he would answer that we could only see *one* pole of the Party's thinking, whereas he knew the *other* pole too and had to take both equally into account. He seemed like a man caught between two clashing rocks who prays to one of them to keep still and save him from being crushed by the other. Those Congress speeches had made it harder than ever for him to fulfil his mission. In the 'ideologically integrated core' of the Party it was he who was responsible for the cultural sector: now it was being said that he had failed to do his job. From Havlíček's peculiar angle it must indeed have seemed that it was not the speakers themselves who were responsible for everything said at the Congress, but solely the head of the Party's Ideological Department and the corresponding member of the Central Committee Secretariat. One could sense the vision —by no means fantastic—that haunted him: the vision of Comrade Number One looking straight through the meaningless puppets on the Congress platform and fixing his gaze directly on the two men who were answerable to Him for the whole Ideological Front. For whom, after all, does the Supreme Commander call to account when things go wrong? Not the corporal who misreported the enemy's position, but the general next to himself in rank.

It is one of the commonest forms of self-deception amongst otherwise honest men of goodwill to imagine they are achieving something by urging moderation on one side in a conflict, on the grounds that too radical a position will only injure that side's interests and antagonise the other so much that a situation, now just tolerable, will be aggravated beyond bearing. This was a popular calculation at the time we are speaking of, but a basically false one. It never yielded a correct solution to any problem, but only a host of bogus moral dilemmas, chronically arrested crises and delusively soothing prescriptions for the treatment of fear, bad conscience and—to give it its right name—plain cowardice.

It was a calculation that never worked when one side of the conflict was in various ways looking for the truth, while all the power was concentrated on the other. By preaching peace to one side the advocate (so frequent a figure in our country) of compromise, or rather of the 'middle way', is really serving the interests of the other, whatever he may think. When the unremitting tensions finally, after many timid postponements, make a showdown inevitable, the man in the middle is either forced into open support of the side that wields power or is unkindly pushed aside as useless, however aggrieved and misjudged he feels.

This must have been roughly what Procházka thought of Havlíček's sermon; his way of expressing it, though perhaps less analytical, was a great deal livelier. Havlíček immediately took offence to the point of gathering up his papers as if to leave, even though it was his own office and we were the visitors. Procházka managed with a great effort, however, to suppress his natural aggressiveness toward a man for whom he felt no respect. When he had given some assurance that the interview would not be a slanging match, and only then, Havlíček calmed down too and we were able to proceed to work.

And laborious work it was. To be truthful we were at that moment prepared to give way over the printing of Kohout's and Vaculík's speeches, and even to surrender Klíma, Havel and Liehm, as long as we could get agreement to publish Novomeský and Milan Kundera. Even that would have been such an event, such a breach in the wall of silence, that it would hardly have failed to launch a public discussion which would make the publication of further Congress speeches irresistible. Perhaps we were wrong, but that is how it seemed to us at the time. In any case we felt ourselves amateurs in the business of negotiation and if we were trying to be diplomatic it was only in imitation of the professionals opposite.

The worthy Ladislav Novomeský is probably unaware even today what a bone of contention his Congress speech had become, what arguments we produced to prove its publication necessary and what arguments they threw back at us to prove it impossible. Pursuing the speculative logic of conflict we made concessions so as to enable our opponent to make them too. But whenever our

positions grew closer and the possibility of a compromise appeared
on the horizon, chief censor Kovařík would emerge from his
silence and start invoking his 'executive' ghost. At first I assumed
that it was us, the lawbreakers, he was trying to frighten, then I
noticed to my astonishment that the threat was having its effect
on the chief ideologist as well. Whenever the bogey appeared
Havlíček wavered and went into reverse, returning to his original
position at the start of the interview. Once or twice he made an
effort to stampede the censor and his bogey, even shouting out
on one occasion that 'we' were not going to let 'them' tell us
what we could or couldn't do; but he never had the courage to
ignore what Kovařík was saying. It was instructive to see on
this and other occasions what authority the censorship had
acquired. Created to be an instrument of the Party centre's will,
its very inertia enabled it on the contrary to influence the *apparat*
at moments when it would have been opportune for it to proceed
more skilfully and to deviate for tactical purposes from its own
rules. But the Party could not shake the incubus off, even when
it dragged like a weight around its legs.

Novomeský's speech had dealt in the main with the harmful
effects of censorship. The chief censor would not let us go
beyond a vague agreement that the remaining, and shorter,
portion of the speech, concerning Czech-Slovak relations, could
be printed while the rest could only appear in the form of an
editorial introduction in which we should say in our own words
what Novomeský had been talking about and what his view was.
I could already envisage the endless struggle awaiting us, for
even if we were allowed to write such an introduction the
censor's office would have the last word in deciding how much
of it could be printed.

The next item on the agenda was Kundera's piece. Kundera,
as I have said, was a difficult customer. For a long time he had
refused even to acknowledge the existence of the Central Publications Board, and with fastidious perseverance he had avoided
any meetings or dealings with its staff. As a result, his manuscripts
for the most part failed to get published. Even in cases where the
censor only asked for minor changes and the damage could be
kept to a minimum with a little skilful editing, Kundera would
refuse either to perform the operation himself or to let an editor

do it for him: he would rather take his copy back and once more forgo publication.

We often remonstrated with him over this because the editors then had the problem of finding an alternative article, and in any case it was a pity that everything he wrote should have to lie fallow because of some triviality. But Kundera's rather eccentric consistency bore surprising fruit. As the censor's officials came to realise that their slightest interference would eliminate the whole text and bring a shower of complaints from our side, they became much more reluctant to meddle. When they felt that some article of Kundera's was on the fringe of permissibility they would often turn a blind eye and refrain from taking a step whose effect, on their own admission, would be petty in relation to the whole. In this way Kundera procured for himself, albeit at a high price, slightly more dignified treatment than was normal. And by making the officials nervous and unsure of their ground he also protected his work from the kind of stylistic and structural disfigurement that usually resulted from the hasty alterations made to meet their demands.

The text of Kundera's Congress speech lay before us on the table. A red pencil had gone over the proof sheet, marking what the censors required to be excised before it could appear in print. The changes were indeed scandalous; they would have left nothing but a pathetic skeleton, devoid of logic. We were required to leave out passages so vital that the gaps would have yawned like toothless mouths.

Kundera knew about the proposed cuts beforehand from an editorial meeting where he had told the visiting representative of the Ideological Department that he would rather forbid publication altogether than accept them. Today, he started off on a note of mild but astonished indignation. He failed to understand why anything at all should be omitted from his speech, and he was against cuts on principle. This was consistent enough with his previous attitude, and also with the assumption that even the Ideological Department would be reluctant just then to embark on too conspicuous a quarrel with the writers. Only recently Havlíček himself had published an article in the Party's theoretical monthly *Nová mysl*, a strange apologia in which he had tried to draw a distinction between a few 'extremists' and the writers as a whole, while stressing the value of certain other contributions at the Congress which had supported the official line and in some fashion redounded to the credit of Havlíček's own department. He had sought to give the impression that most writers accepted the line and would be able to back it all the more effectively if only the good start made at the Congress were continued and the 'extremists' pushed aside. This defensive interpretation could not have been sustained in face of the open rift which failure to publish any record of the Congress would have brought about.

Clearly, then, Havlíček had not altogether set his mind against concessions; his very willingness to meet us showed this. And whether or not any of the Congress speeches were to be published in *Literární noviny* now depended for all practical purposes on his ability to come to terms with Kundera. Knowing this, Kundera in turn insisted that his contribution to the Congress had been a thoroughly thought-out and carefully constructed essay in which he could not change a single word. If for any reason the Ideological Department felt it contained passages unsuitable for publication, then none of it should appear.

The situation then was that far from our defending Kundera's treatise it was our opponents who were having to defend their own encroachments and explain why they had objected to this or that passage. There were some remarks, for example, about the film *Sedmikrásky (The Daisies)*. Kundera had been much taken with the parable of 'two gloriously repulsive girls, smugly satisfied with their own delightful mediocrity and gaily wrecking everything that transcended their horizon'. Vandalism, he had argued, crops up not only in individuals, when it is generally abhorred—as in the young lout who knocks heads off statues in a park—but also in a social form with long lasting effects. The representatives of the public, for example, may vote to have not only the statues removed but the nearby castle, church and centuries-old lime-tree, on the grounds that they are all 'superfluous'. Kundera had then added the following general reflection which the censor wanted removed.

There is basically no difference between legal and illegal destruction, between destruction and prohibition. A Czech deputy recently asked in Parliament on behalf of twenty-one other deputies for the prohibition of two serious and intelligent Czech films. One of them, ironically, was this parable of the vandals, *Sedmikrásky*. He inveighed savagely against both films, while positively boasting that he understood neither of them. The contradiction in such an attitude is only on the surface. The two works had chiefly offended by transcending the human horizons of their judges, so that they were felt as an insult.

Kundera would not have this cut. His only reason for quoting examples of hooliganism, he argued, was to show the relation between the actions of hooligans and the actions of society or of the authorities. Otherwise he would not have mentioned them. He was not writing a tract against adolescent delinquency in parks; he was not a crime reporter for an evening paper. Havlíček answered that he was not so much concerned with the factual side of the matter; the complaint in Parliament had not been at all to the liking of progressive people like himself in the Party Secretariat who were having their own struggle against extreme attitudes. But if their efforts were to have any success they must have a calm atmosphere to operate in; any public furore would jeopardise them.

Kundera would have nothing of this perverse logic. It was the first time in Czech history, he went on, that a Czech politician had demanded the suppression of a Czech work of art; silence was no way to win the fight against such impudence. He asked what reason there could be to refrain from criticising the deputy, when something had to be protected from the deputy's criticism.

At this point we were given to understand that Havlíček was not merely up against the insignificant person of the deputy in question, Pružinec, but also against several important members of the Party Presidium who had discussed the film in terms similar to those used in Parliament. Possibly, indeed, the most important of all the Presidium members was involved. The censor's mind clearly boggled at the thought of criticising, even by implication, Antonín Novotný himself.

Hearing this revelation Kundera simply shrugged his shoulders and agreed that the passage should be withheld—along with the rest of the article. There was no particular need, he added, for it to be printed today or in a month's time. The day would come when publication was possible; Kundera would bide his time.

Now it was Havlíček himself who tried to find some way of restoring the banned paragraph, but he only got as far as querying the 'generalisation' of the vandalism issue, which was itself painful enough for the authorities at that time. Kundera promptly protested that unless the generalisation stayed the whole previous argument was pointless and would have to go too. However, that passage led organically to the next theme, the need to seek truth by a dialogue between opposed views on a free and equal basis. And this was precisely the next place where the censor's pencil had fallen.

> Any interference with freedom of thought and word, how-ever discreet the mechanics and terminology of such censorship, is a scandal in this century, a chain entangling the limbs of our national literature as it tries to bound forward.

The cut after that began as follows:

> In our society it is counted a greater virtue to guard the frontiers than to cross them. The most transitory political and social considerations are used to justify all kinds of con-straint on our intellectual liberty. But great policies are policies that set the interest of the age above the interest of the moment. The quality of Czech culture is, for the Czech nation, the interest of a whole epoch.

Kundera strongly defended this passage and again insisted that if it were to be dropped the whole piece should be abandoned. He kept on raising the discussion to a level far above the horse-trading at which our opponents were so adept. Again and again he pointed to the absurdity of censoring a text that protested against all censorship. The other side had no arguments at hand to cope with this; their only technique for ensuring victory would have been to cut the discussion short and issue an order. But they were not in a position to give Kundera orders.

Word by word, sentence by sentence, Havlíček beat his

retreat. As soon as it was clear that the whole passage about vandalism and *Sedmikrásky* could stay, Kundera agreed to modify a few phrases. But each proposed alternative horrified him; he protested that he could not be expected on the spur of the moment to find another expression to replace one he had spent so much time searching for in the first place. Havlíček accordingly suggested that he sat apart from us for a while and tried polishing up the insertions in peace and quiet. Anyone familiar with Kundera's habits, his constant rewriting of manuscripts, his requests for changes phoned in at the last minute from Brno and his subsequent lamentations when he saw the result, can imagine how delighted he was at this proposal for a rapid revision 'in peace'. I still have the pages that emerged from this melancholy labour. The reader will see, alongside the censor's straight lines, drawings of hideously misshapen cripples and weird primitive faces—not illustrations, but subconscious by-products of what was going on in Kundera's mind. Some of the sentences have been crossed out and replaced by fresh ones, then these in turn crossed out until, word by word, the author returned by devious routes to his original version. For example, the sentence starting

Any interference with freedom of thought and word, however discreet the mechanics and terminology of such censorship . . .

emerged after much revamping as

All interference with freedom of thought and word, however discreet . . .

and so on.

Next we turned our attention to a long passage—really the core of the whole essay—where Kundera portrays the destiny of his nation, tossed between democracy, fascism, stalinism and socialism, and made more painful by the presence of an unparalleled nationality problem. Yet he concludes that the miraculous touch of art can transmute this bitter fate into a unique opportunity: unique not only for art, but for the nation too. (The conclusion explained why Kundera had started his essay by drawing a comparison with that other epoch when art and nation were identified—the National Rebirth in the nineteenth century.)

The collision was now a very fundamental one. For a while we fought over the term *stalinism* which, the censors insisted, belonged to the vocabulary of anti-communist propaganda and was therefore inadmissible. After a lot of hesitation Kundera agreed to replace it with *stalinist dogmatism*, but nothing else. Again he was on the point of getting up and leaving and again this would not have suited Havlíček's plans. So the Party ideologist, hedged in between the long arm of the Ministry of the Interior on one side and an adamant Kundera on the other, had a shot at dictating a revised version of the offending sentence himself. Years ago Havlíček had been a secondary schoolteacher, but his style was now marked by a bureaucratic glibness, conveying everything and nothing at the same time while avoiding any breach of the current line.

This move incensed Kundera and, since he was already losing his patience, I was alarmed to think what he might do next. Though I had originally intended to keep out of this particular argument I felt it necessary to hold him firmly down in his seat. We were so near to the finish that it would have been a pity to end up quarrelling. So I proposed a wording which did little damage to Kundera's text and with any luck would be acceptable to the censors. It was.

And so finally we had achieved a version of the Kundera speech which preserved its sense, its reasoning, its structure and style. The concessions were only in points of detail, interesting though these were, and I felt we must swallow our losses. Our opponents had retreated much further than we had, and in far more substantial matters. It had been a compromise, but a surprisingly successful one.

Should we have been pleased?

I was not so sure. We did not pay much attention when Havlíček wound up with the remark that his authority was limited and he would have to check with his superiors before our agreement became valid. I was wondering whether we for our part had not exceeded our competence, whether our compromise would find favour with the editorial board and how the Writers' Union and the general public would react. My own feeling was that we had given way too much over the Novomeský piece. Novomeský was not around to give an opinion, but Kundera, as he strode along the Vltava embankment with us, was racked with misgivings.

'Why did I knuckle under? . . . I let them make a complete idiot of me . . . Vaculík's quite right when he says every compromise is a dirty compromise . . .'

6
Censorship:
facts are forbidden

No sooner had we reached the *Literární noviny* offices than I was called to the telephone. The Party Central Committee wanted me. It was Havlíček on the line to tell me he had now consulted with the appropriate quarters and was very sorry, but none of the agreements we had made was acceptable. He had to go back to his original request both in regard to the Novomeský and to the Kundera. I asked him if he realised that in that case *Literární noviny* would have no option but to publish nothing at all for the time being about the Congress, and to leave the whole matter to the Writers' Union and its committee to deal with—whenever the committee was able to meet. Yes, he had realised that.

So our whole tedious negotiation might never have taken place. Its total result: zero. All I had gained from it was Kundera's text with its desperate insertions and gruesome figures, and the painful insight they conveyed.

But Kundera was most relieved by the news.

'Right, that's fine! Now I feel a lot better.'

Procházka's comment was chilly.

'Well, *they* took the decision. This means war.'

If the afternoon's activity had achieved anything useful it was to disprove the charge that *Literární noviny* had refused to print a record of the Congress because of some cliquish intolerance toward writers outside its own group. When Havlíček made this claim a few months later at a Party fraction meeting of the Union's committee it was easy to refute it by giving the bare facts of what transpired at today's meeting. In their effort to demonstrate goodwill the paper's editors may have conceded too much, but the trouble lay palpably with the shortage of goodwill on the other side.

With Kohout, Vaculík, Klíma, Havel and Liehm all totally expunged from the record, Novomeský three-quarters suppressed, Kundera bowdlerised and many other speakers heavily pruned, what was really left of the Congress proceedings? There were further contributions whose authors would not allow them to be printed as long as their colleagues remained under the ban. So that left just Pludek, Šuleř, Skála, Hájek and Lajčiak, whose speeches under the original agreement would anyway have appeared alongside the others. We felt we could happily leave these, in the circumstances, to be put out by some other paper which had no objection to onesided reporting. Shortly afterwards some of these were in fact published by the Party daily, *Rudé právo*.

It might seem from our account as if the censors had only been suppressing the efforts of writers and that the whole wearisome struggle had been a strictly literary and journalistic affair of no special interest to the man-in-the-street who has never tried to get anything published or had anything confisciated by the Central Publications Board. In reality, however, I think it is not too much to say that the effects of censorship were of equal, indeed of primary, interest to the general public. I shall try, therefore, to supplement what I have said about the censor's confiscations in regard to the Writers' Congress with some remark on his depredations in other and far more important fields which the Congress only mirrored from afar.

Our censors were in fact a great deal less interested in purely literary matters than the reader might think from what we have said. The works of Franz Kafka, Albert Camus, Eugène Ionesco and their followers in Czechoslovakia, all representatives of 'rotten, degenerate bourgeois pseudo-art', made little impression on the eagle-eyed guardians of socialist doctrine as long as there was no intrusion into current public affairs. To this extent the policies of the Party centre were genuinely 'liberal'—and were indeed regarded as highly blasphemous by the still more dogmatic guardians of thought in, for example, that glasshouse of inviolable orthodoxy, the German Democratic Republic. Literature that either ignored current events or only passed obscure or indirect judgement on them was given a certain genuine scope for development. But even the most introspective schools of writing cannot flourish for long on internal resources alone. All literature must sooner or later feel the need and duty to explore and examine reality, to distinguish between the authentic and the false; and the more symptoms of stagnation, deceit and hypocrisy multiply in a society, the more compulsively that need and duty are felt.

If such reactions are inevitable in literature generally, they are the very lifeblood of journalism which, without them, denies its own nature and degenerates into the trivialities of the gutter press. Among the various cultural crafts it is the role of journalism to penetrate into the unknown, to discover new areas of progress and to do this with speed and agility, accepting the inevitable risks of superficiality and error. There are plenty of natural impediments to be overcome for those who engage in such activity—the inertia of the human mind that clings to old certainties and resents novelty; national traditions and myths; conventional morality; class barriers, and so forth. But the continuous conflict of ideas is the setting in which the national community, like the European and world communities, pursues its evolution.

The degree of foresight of those politicians who, in acquiring power from time to time, also assume leadership in national affairs, can be judged *inter alia* by their ability to reconcile the requirements of everyday government with that other need—continuously to acquaint themselves with the wider issues and more general trends of social change. The practical politician may often feel at odds with those who take the broader view, will think their criticisms unfair and resent them for casting doubt on the correctness of policies he has never queried. He will certainly be forever tempted to silence the critic or at least to curtail his liberty of speech: the politician has, after all, the means and the authority. His wisdom is then revealed by the extent to which he resists temptation and by the scope he grants to those engaged in fact-finding—which must include, of course, the quest for self-knowledge. Success in discovering a fruitful relationship between short-term concerns and more general interests is one test of the quality of political leaders and of their fitness to lead. As Milan Kundera put it in his Congress speech:

'Great policies are policies that set the interest of the age above the interest of the moment.'

By the same token one might say that political leaders define themselves, and determine their own scope for development, by the degree of intellectual freedom they permit. The more they restrict it the more firmly they condemn themselves to stagnation. If they completely abolish liberty of self-expression in public— private activities they cannot wholly control—then they consign themselves, sooner or later, to failure and collapse.

Censorship, then, is catastrophic in all directions: for society, for the creative artist, and for the very political leaders who install it.

What in fact was it forbidden to say in our country? This was never openly stated and there were many vague declarations, of course, to the effect that nothing was prohibited at all.

However, *it was in the first place prohibited to describe the state of the national economy, to compare its achievements with those of other countries or to mention its effects on the living standard of the population.* By the time I had read some dozens of articles on these subjects which were not to be published at all, and dozens more which could only be passed for printing with specified cuts, I realised how systematically the barest information was being suppressed: not analyses or proposals but the simplest facts and statistical data without which understanding of the situation was impossible. A typical example of the censor's procedure was his confiscation of a letter from one *Literární noviny* reader, Jiří Dunovský, commenting on a radio talk.

. . . In this otherwise impressive account there was one false note—the reference to living standards in West Germany. True, oranges are cheaper than here, while food in general is twice or three times as dear and rents and especially prices of houses several times higher. But these data are only half the story: what was missing was a comparison of average incomes which are several times larger there than here, perhaps five times. (I will not attempt an exact comparison because such conversions are amongst the most difficult to perform.) Nor was it mentioned that incomes are higher for skilled workers, while on the other hand higher incomes attract higher taxes.

Even a simple empirical observation of this kind, whose correctness was beyond doubt, contradicted the official picture of socialism as superior to capitalism in all respects. In many ways this superiority had not been confirmed in practice. But the authorities were concerned here with suppressing facts, not with evaluating and explaining them. The Czechoslovak public was not allowed to learn the truth from its own press, so that (for example) Svatopluk Pekárek's findings about the housing situation had to remain unpublished: he had ascertained that the chronic shortage of housing was getting gradually worse, whereas the official line was that it was getting gradually better. A similar fate met many of Helena Klímová's studies on the position of women in employment and on the critical state of social provision for children—simply because she had ascertained that welfare problems were not solved by the arrival of a socialist system but acquired new and often alarming forms.

That part of the public which only had official information to draw on was thus kept in ignorance of the real state of affairs. It was encouraged to go on believing that the bureaucratic version of socialism favoured by the authorities was leading the country to a degree of prosperity unequalled by other systems and that it was the best way to banish social injustice. Unable to compare their own living standards with those of foreign countries, and unaware of other approaches to social problems, a section of the population really accepted these illusions. When Notovný later fell from office and Professor Šik was able to reveal the critical state of the economy by quoting sober facts, many people asked: 'Why didn't he tell us this before? Surely he knew?'

Assuredly Šik and many other economists and laymen had known both the general picture and many of the details long before. But they did not state them because they were not allowed to. They were prevented by the Party centre of the day, and by the censorship with which it controlled press, radio and television. *Literární noviny's* collection of articles prohibited over the years contains all the facts about the national economy and living standard which were to shock some readers, and confirm the worst fears of others, when they were later collated and published.

While inconvenient facts were banned as 'unsuitable' or

'negativist', actual criticism of prevailing theory and practice, whether direct or implicit, was dubbed hostile and anti-socialist Thus the public was never allowed to see for example Radoslav Selucký's critique of the cult of the Plan in the centralised command economy, of production for production's sake divorced from the needs of the home and foreign market, of technical backwardness even in new factories etc. Alarmed by facts which contradicted their claims, the authorities felt still more threatened by comments which stressed their responsibility. They suppressed the one and the other for so many years that in the end they seem to have adopted the philosophy of *après nous le déluge*. In this again they were assisted by the censor's ability to keep the bulk of the public uninformed, or scantily informed.

It was also forbidden to say what people's political rights really were, what share they could claim in running public affairs and what their position as citizens was. The pre-1968 political model was a worthy counterpart to the sagging economy. Economic and political conditions affected each other reciprocally: *dirigiste* political ideas determined the form of the economy, which in turn provoked discriminatory measures in the political field. It was not permitted to publish the findings of sociological surveys, confirmed in countless readers' letters and routine observations by reporters, to the effect that the working class in whose name the Party centre ruled had in fact lost the political rights it had fought for for a century, lost real political influence and lost the chance to share in forming and executing Party or state policy. On every rung of the ladder the working class was represented by paid officials of Party, state or government whose main feature was that they were convinced, or at least obedient, executives of the centre's instructions. The workers were led by their autocratic spokesmen into a state of political servility and often into dire social straits as well, so that they were sometimes on the brink of revolt. *Literární noviny* reporters collected a great deal of information about the working and social conditions of men and women employees in light industry. But their testimony was not allowed to be published. Nor, naturally, was it possible to print evidence of the material and moral corruption which had befallen those élite sectors of the working class on whom the Party centre continued to rely for its chief support. Often enough it was only official demagogy, playing upon proletarian pride, which turned the workers' anger away from those actually responsible for their plight and directed it at bogus culprits like the writers and 'similar elements'. By swallowing such propaganda the workers only prolonged the rule of the existing Power centre over themselves and intensified their humiliation. Proposals that the trade unions should start seriously defending working class interests remained hidden in well-locked drawers; ideas that the workers' organisation should be democratised, or that employees should share in running their enterprises, were treated as well-nigh treasonable.

It was not allowed to criticise decisions made by bureaucratic institutions against the interests of private citizens, since this was regarded as an attack on popular self-government (from which the 'popular' element had been long eliminated). One could not even report cases of notorious injustice committed by the authorities against people in the people's name. Even when local, and especially district, level officials overstepped the mark and perpetrated acts of terror or caprice, they could use their influence with the Party to silence the critics and any disciplinary decisions were made behind closed doors. 'Comrade X may have overdone it this time, but he's a reliable man with a good record, and he's one of us. Surely we shouldn't dispense with a man like that? If things get too noticeable we'll transfer him elsewhere.'

The confiscated material in the archives of our paper alone contains dozens of reports, terrible to read, of basic civil rights being violated, lives ruined, frustrated or uprooted, persecution continuing over many years—cries of despair from people unable to secure justice and forced to live and die with a sense of intolerable wrong.

Even vague references to this kind of evil were finally forbidden. In an article by Jiří Lederer on conditions in one country village we had to remove a phrase quoted from a schoolmistress: 'Everyone is afraid of everyone else . . .' And the following passage had to be excised from the monologue of a local Party branch chairman:

You know, I keep wondering what sort of people we communists really are. What is it that makes us better, different and all that? Is it our work? Or our characters? Or our knowledge? I know a lot of people outside the Party who are better in all those ways. Anyway, what is it that makes us communists? Having a Party card? Paying our dues? Going to meetings? Obeying the rules? I know all about the 'mission of the Party', but what I keep asking myself about now is ourselves, the individuals. Aren't our Party cards perhaps just passports to better jobs and earlier salary increases in reward for our 'work', our 'character', our 'knowledge'? And aren't they sometimes the *only* passports to these things? . . .

It was the function of the censorship as the long arm of the Party authorities to protect the public from this kind of moral misgiving, to prevent the well fed from hearing about the starving, or the powerful from being alarmed about the weak, to still people's consciences and divert their attention from matters of common interest.

One could go on quoting examples indefinitely: hundreds of articles were confiscated, thousands of passages removed from the remainder. The demand that 'shops should oblige their customers and not the other way round' was barred as an attack on the socialist distribution network and therefore an indirect attack on socialism itself. The outstanding Slovak academician O. Pavlík was not allowed to publish his thoughts about the deficiencies of the school system in *Literární noviny* because the school reforms had been part of socialism and must not be criticised. Even notoriously justified complaints about the functioning of communal services were ultimately hushed up on the grounds that they constituted an 'underhand attack on the rule of the working class', hard though it might be to see how the working class could benefit from inefficient services.

Whenever anything of a critical nature appeared in print, it was only after tedious and painful argument. Now and again the Party centre did allow notes of discontent to be heard, in order that great improvements could then be claimed; or it permitted criticism to be made so that an inconvenient official could be removed and replaced by someone more loyal to the official line. Such personnel changes, however, were not due to objective circumstances but to the whims of the Party centre, which often took a dislike to a man and sacrificed him accordingly. One of the nastiest aspects of the system was that even justified criticism was distorted so as to pin responsibility on to local officials for 'misunderstanding' or 'inefficiently executing' central directives—whence the recurrent stories attributing the whole nation's ills to, say, the Party District Secretary in Kladno. Plenty of the system's servants failed in their tasks, but nobody was allowed to ask the question, Were they not *bound* to fail in a system created by the rulers of that period? The censor's purpose was to create an appearance of infallibility on the rulers' part, and what limited criticism was allowed served the function (whether the critics liked it or not) of bolstering up the façade of a democratically functioning society and the rulers' reputation for wisdom and benevolence.

There was one subject, however, on which the censor's ban was absolute and no concession could be won by persuasion or defiance. *The strictest of all taboos applied to the political trials of the 'fifties and after, to the judicial murders that ensued from them and to everything that lay behind them.* Following the Soviet Twentieth Congress the knowledge, or at least some suspicion, of the criminal character of those trials was no longer limited to a small circle. There were a great many people thinking about it and passionately demanding the full truth, even if their voices were consistently drowned. There were historians and research students who managed here and there to penetrate into forgotten archives and uncover fragments of evidence about what had really happened, though what they discovered could only be passed on by word of mouth or read in unpublished manuscripts. The families of the victims, feeling they had nothing more to lose, gradually ceased being afraid to speak about what their relatives had endured and what they themselves had suffered. Slovak spokesmen in particular, wounded in their national pride by the trials of so-called 'Slovak bourgeois nationalists', started to break down the wall of silence. They were the first to secure the rehabilitation of the survivors and they brought about the fall of Viliam Široký and others responsible for the false charges—men whom Novotný was happy to sacrifice in order to atone for his own sins. This process enabled a large number of people to gain glimpses of the hidden background to the trials, and from their first horror arose a determination to decode the mysteries and expose everything to the light of truth. The threads of guilt and of political association alike led in one direction—to highly placed personalities of the Party centre and most clearly to the highest placed of all, Comrade Number One. Finally the general crisis that hit the country, a crisis largely attributable to the Party centre's actions, demonstrated the continuity of the regime's political, administrative and power-imposing methods despite the abandonment of the worst extremes. Innocent trial victims, in so far as they had escaped the gallows, began to emerge from the prisons and in some cases were not afraid to tell their stories. The very hesitation and tight-lipped half-heartedness of their rehabilitation betrayed the uneasy consciences of the ruling group and showed up both their responsibility for what had been done and their failure to abolish the practices of the past.

One of the worst scandals in the history of *Literární noviny* was that involving an article by the historian Milan Hübl who, in the purgative atmosphere after the Twentieth Congress, gave some thought to that political tendency in the communist movement illustrated by the Soviet trials of the 1930's. The resultant article said, or hinted, a certain amount about the analogous problem in our own history. That it could be published at all is evidence of the general thaw and wide-ranging discussion of that period, reminiscent in many ways of the later movement that culminated in the Central Committee plenum of January 1968. Shortly after publication of this article, however, Hübl was dismissed from the post of vice-rector of the Party High School and relegated to a subordinate function along with several of his colleagues. A fierce private campaign was then launched against *Literární noviny*, some sparks from which were noticed by the public. There were many and various charges against the paper, but it was never admitted what the real issue was, namely the official untouchability of the old political trials and their contemporary ramifications. From that moment on, *Literární noviny* was continually checked and harried and subjected to special rulings. But the chief concern of the censors and the subject of their sternest proscriptions was that no single line should be printed about the trials or any questions connected with them.

I had a number of sad experiences in this field myself. I was never able to publish more than a bare historical reference to the issue, as if it were some self-contained episode belonging wholly to the past. The censorship officials would react to every argument by shrugging their shoulders and invoking their instructions. They knew something about the subject, whether from texts they had themselves confiscated or from other sources. But they were not allowed to use their knowledge as a guide and they knew they might be called to account for what they let pass, but never for what they held up. The function of the machinery they formed part of was not to encourage thought and creativeness, but to supervise the constraints upon thought and creativeness, and they were not selected for their education or sense of justice but for their knowledge of the rules and ability to see them meticulously adhered to. A censor who happened to have been at school with me told me on one occasion with evident sincerity how sorry he was to have to reject a piece I had written, though he himself could see nothing objectionable in it.

At another time I was asked by the editors of *Sešity pro mladou literaturu* what I would publish if I were in their position, and was offered two pages in their own journal to put out a text of my own choice. Knowing that the censors would not tolerate any political analysis or comment on the subject, I chose an extract from the official record of the Slánský trial, adding a brief footnote about recent evidence on the period. Yet not even then—it was 1967—could anyone print part of an official publication of the Ministry of Justice dating from 1953. The censor pointed out that I was surely aware of his strict terms of reference and accompanied his rejection with this astonishing remark: 'I quite appreciate your feelings and I don't feel happy about doing this to you. If I hadn't given up journalism years ago I'd no doubt be writing the same sort of things myself.'

There was a more serious side to the problem than the moral dilemmas of the individual censors. By maintaining their taboo on the trials they were covering up not only the mistakes of the old Party centre but the partial or sometimes quite direct responsibility of some of its members for judicial murders unprecedented in Czech or Slovak history. It was not just a matter of suppressing criticism but of shielding politicians whose rise and continuance in office were stained by crime.

When later, after January 1969 and Novotný's fall from power, some of the sensational details reached the readers of the press, many of them were indignant even though what were being published were bare facts without any attempt to analyse all the background—*that* had still to be disentangled. Some, surprisingly, were angry with the journalists for printing these things. 'Didn't you know all this before?' they would ask, suspecting us of some obsessive professional interest in the subject.

Some of us had, of course, known a good deal, but the censors had done their best to ensure that this knowledge was restricted to a fairly small circle of people. The belated start that was made finally on uncovering the facts, and the violent emotional reactions of the public, came after years of concealment that prevented any thorough understanding, let alone readiness to settle accounts. For what had to be done was not just to name the culprits and remove them from power but to create guarantees against repetitions and relapses—in public feeling as well as in the political and judicial system. This was not, and will not be, a pleasant operation; for it must inevitably involve a self-critical admission of one's own mistakes, obscured as they have been by the passage of time and the facile excuses and moral clichés of an earlier period.

But whose fault are the embarrassments caused by long-postponed disclosures? Are those to blame who are now dragging the facts out into the light and probing for their causes and their contemporary implications? Or those who did the deeds, kept them hidden and spent years hoodwinking the public—the whole nation, the working class, the Communist Party, and all those in whose name they pretended to be acting?

Censorship was baneful in every sphere, but by helping to cover up crime it had a profound effect on the very roots of the nation's social conscience, character and moral health. I do not suspect the majority of the censorship officials of evil intentions; it is easy for them to prove that they meant well and to justify themselves for showing discipline in executing the orders of a perfectly legal ruling centre. This is just one more sad illustration of how *evil can be abetted by good intentions* and by that much-praised quality of reliability and obedience, above which hovers—in many crucial aspects of twentieth-century experience—a question-mark always liable to turn into an exclamation-mark.

Can it then be maintained that the protracted campaign against the censors, of which *Literární noviny* was the chief battlefield and the Writers' Congress the culminating battle, was a private concern for authors and newspapermen? Was it for them to settle their own quarrel with the Party centre and not involve the general public? Was it just their hypersensitive temperament, their arrogance, greed for privilege, querulousness and thirst for sensation that led them into revolt and earned them labels like 'anti-state', 'anti-Party' and 'anti-socialist'?

If the writers had been fighting for their alleged privileges, or even primarily for their own professional interests, it is not the censorship they would have rebelled against but the royalty arrangements which make the Czechoslovak author one of the worst-rewarded in Europe and the socialist world. They would have directed their main fire against a tax law which victimises them in a fashion scarcely any other social group would tolerate, a tax law inflicted on them as punishment for their refusal to accept the ruling doctrines and practice of the time and accompanied by a promise that the burden would be relieved once they agreed to give the authorities their support. They would have raised their voices against such legal theft as the system, unparalleled elsewhere, by which the state pocketed sixty per cent of all hard-currency royalties earned abroad and gave the author a derisory equivalent in domestic currency. (With all this writers were being continually accused of living 'on state accounts' and 'at the workers' expense', though in fact they supported only themselves by their earnings while their publishers paid millions of crowns into the state's coffers every year.)

I am aware of the mixed feelings and confused impressions the public entertains on this subject, but the facts have to be mentioned for the light they throw on the writers' 'professional interests'— about which, incidentally, not a word was said at the Congress, nor did they feature as a bone of contention with the authorities of the day.

The only bone of contention was the system of censorship as a cardinal element in the theory and practice of ruling and as a means of stopping criticism of stalinist, bureaucratic socialism. It was censorship which was making it impossible to talk about or to understand the plight and prospects of the country's economy, the effective elimination of the working class from political decision-making, its material abasement and deprivation of civic rights. It was censorship which forbade discussion or comprehension of the way in which institutions set up to serve the public had been turned into instruments of control over the public on behalf of the omnipotent authorities. It was censorship which concealed the process by which the functioning of a bureaucratic police state fostered boorishness and bullying, shielded mediocrity, stifled initiative, drove people into apathy and prevented them from discovering the basic truth that injustice and happiness are incompatible. Censorship made it impermissible even to ask the question, Is the system we are moving towards a socialist system at all? And censorship made the crimes of some of our leading figures an unmentionable topic.

None of these were narrow professional issues for men of letters. Men of letters were certainly prevented by censorship from publicising their own concerns, but they were also, and more importantly, prevented from saying what was in the public interest. To have pointed out the public interest would not have been any special feat of altruism on their part; it was their obvious duty. If they joined the struggle for freedom of thought it was as part of a wider freedom, and they committed themselves as part of a wider public. Literary freedom cannot be achieved at the expense of other freedoms; it is a bitter thing to learn, and yet a fine thing, that it can be won only in conjunction with the social and civil freedom of everyone.

This fact was by no means perceived overnight; awareness of it matured over a period of years, thanks to the way in which society was developing and, in the last resort, to the attitude of the authorities themselves. There is an interesting relationship between two factors here: the curve of social insight is closely accompanied by the curve of censorship, which normally hangs behind but leaps into the lead at every violent turn of events when political upset seems to threaten. This is not due to any diabolical malice on the part of the censors themselves: they merely reflect the demands and mentality of the ruling élite, whose instrument they are but whom they in turn influence this way or that in choosing options between repression on the one hand and manipulation on the other.

Some years ago I reproached one of the Deputy Ministers of the Interior, whose portfolio included the censor's office, with the damaging and nonsensical activities carried out in his sphere. He snapped back at me:

'Why tell me this? You ought to tell Hendrych!'

It was inherent in the logic and evolution of the old system that, regardless of the formal demarcation of responsibility, everything was run by the Party centre, which gradually came to trust nobody outside itself and in the end nobody inside either, except for Comrade Number One. After the 1948 takeover the country's political leaders had no great difficulties; movement towards socialism followed naturally from the nation's social development and was sincerely endorsed by the majority. Those who opposed it, or even then saw symptoms of incipient deformation, went abroad or were condemned to silence as 'internal émigrés', voluntarily or in a more literal sense. The leaders felt assured of majority support even after they had abandoned the 'specific road to socialism', as shown by the crucial Cominform resolution on Yugoslavia in 1948. It is rather discouraging nowadays to read the newspapers of that time and the statements of leading artists and writers. But it will serve as a warning lesson now that Czechoslovak policies have come round full circle to a revised version of the 'specific road' and are attracting from certain socialist leaders abroad a response which sounds like a revised version of the excommunication of Tito.

When Tito was being described in our press as a 'bloodstained cur' and no word could be published in his defence, when our own spokesmen of the 'specific road' were being executed as imperialist agents or Titoist spies, or else being broken by threats and turned into willing tools of stalinism, one basic fact was lost in that welter of fraudulent propaganda. It was this: that the wheel of our own ship had been turned round and we were steering obediently towards the stalinist model of socialism and everything that went with it. In those days it was the writers themselves who were their own best censors; the few who thought differently never offered their works for publication—indeed never committed them to paper in most cases. For it was unthinkable that any discordant voice should raise itself. The Party's accumulated credit, deriving amongst other things from Munich, the German occupation, the liberation and its socialist outcome, was enough to finance even this bad investment with its tragic consequences. In exercising its leading role the Party did not yet need to keep a watch on its own members. It confidently 'deployed its cadres'; for it had enough faithful and reliable men and to spare. In those days the voice of *Literární noviny* provided a decorative accompaniment to the close harmony of the rest of the chorus, whose loyal tones are remembered today with sentimental nostalgia by some, and bitter embarrassment by others. It was an age when the paper had no trouble with the censors, since the censors had no trouble with the paper.

The first discordant notes broke into this idyll after the Soviet Communist Party's Twentieth Congress. The inexorable disclosure of Stalin's crimes and perversions, without which the communist movement would have marched with superb discipline straight over the edge of the cliff, sentencing to death by atomic destruction not only itself and the Soviet Union but the whole world, triggered off a train of thought and awareness which survived even the 'ten days that shook Poland' in 1956, and the notorious Hungarian episode of the same year. But the Czechoslovak Party centre, in which Novotný had already worked his way to the top, managed to dilute the cleansing stream and finally by a mixture of intrigue and fiat to divert it into a different and acceptable course, fondly hoping that the public eye would never see below the surface of its muddy waters. It was at about this point that a new class of men began to appear in editorial offices everywhere: courteous and modest officials transferred from some other place, who now occupied seats in discreet, unpretentious rooms near to the heart of the publishing process, reading and placing their stamps on the proofsheets and occasionally visiting the editor-in-chief for a confidential chat. After such a chat the editor-in-chief would give instructions for this article to be dropped, or a deletion made in that one, as it had always been his prerogative to do. By such quiet, inconspicuous steps did censorship inveigle itself into our daily routine that even working journalists failed to notice it, let alone the public at large. The anonymous way it developed is one of Stalin's great contributions to the enrichment of socialism.

As a further stage, the shortcomings of the censoring procedure were remedied by the creation, by confidential government decree, of the Main Board of Press Control (*Hlavní správa tiskového dohledu*); this was formally subordinate to the Ministry of the Interior, but it was obvious where it actually took its orders from. The Constitution had solemnly declared censorship inadmissible and no new law on the subject had gone through Parliament. True, the authorities of the day took little notice either of the Constitution or of Parliament. All the same, the fewer people knew about it the better. So an institution came into being which had no brass plate outside its headquarters and whose officials sported no visiting cards on their office doors. Indeed their operations grew more obscure and secretive as their responsibilities increased.

No country, of course, turns the searchlight of publicity on its censors and their work. But stalinist socialism tried to conceal their existence altogether, and did so all the more energetically as their activities increasingly conflicted with official protestations that there was more and more freedom, and that harmony prevailed between the interests of state and people. To this day I cannot tell whether the methods of censorship that evolved in our country were based on any carefully weighed previous experience or represented a new addition to the sum of knowledge. At all events it was characterised not only by the bureaucratic brutality normal under stalinism, but also by a certain hypocritical slyness and calm pretence that nothing was amiss. These traits, I fear, represent the Czech contribution to the subject.

The censors, I must explain, never scored anything out or confiscated it themselves. They merely drew attention to points, or conveyed representations. In the early stages, especially, they behaved amiably and correctly; if the other side disagreed with them, they regretted that their competence was so limited and welcomed it if an author or editor appealed, at his own wish or at their instigation, to higher authority. It was not often that 'higher' meant the relevant ministry or competent state official. Since the point at issue was usually ideological, the higher authority was the *apparat* of the Communist Party's Central Committee. If someone could be found there who would approve the text in question and was not afraid of his superiors, a brief communication was enough to win the censor's smile and a stamp on the proofsheet. In the course of time, then, it was the machinery of the Central Committee which took over the job of censorship and of arbitration in censorship matters, like so much else.

However, the number of Central Committee officials willing to endorse contested manuscripts became fewer and fewer as those who showed too much complaisance were reprimanded for 'not standing on points of principle' and replaced by more trustworthy men. Those who had reprimanded them would also ensure that the censors who allowed the original appeal were reprimanded by *their* superiors, and were provided with lists of Central Committee officials authorised to act in connection with various subjects; it was then useless to obtain a favourable ruling from any but these functionaries, who were hard to reach and harder to impress.

Should an editor-in-chief be so convinced of the correctness and value of his material that, having failed to clear all the hurdles of this complex and slow-working machinery he decided to go ahead and publish nevertheless, all the good manners would disappear and everything was reduced to the question, Who gives orders to whom? It would become rapidly clear that an editor-in-chief's authority was purely nominal and that the sole result of such an act of defiance would be the entertainment of serious doubts about his suitability for the post and the threat of dismissal if the Party centre so decided. The printers were in any case forbidden to print anything not bearing the censor's stamp of approval, and this they adhered to. The editor's authority was thus effectively subordinated to that of the censor who, though he could not decide what was to appear, most certainly decided what was not to.

To add to the editor-in-chief's humiliation, however, he was not allowed to leave any blank spaces where an article or a passage had been withdrawn. The censors would make sure that other, and suitable, material was substituted and would refuse to stamp the final proofs until every trace of the change had been erased. Uninitiated members of the public therefore had no notion of the censor's existence, let alone of his high rate of negative output. The astute inventors of this grotesque state of affairs could well be pleased; to all outward appearances there was no censorship, and yet it functioned admirably; nothing, strictly speaking, was banned and yet no undesirable articles appeared; texts were blanked out as the censor's heart desired, yet not a single gap appeared in the pages of books or the columns of newspapers. The public could sleep soundly; for the censorship, which concealed so much else, concealed itself best of all. It was a halcyon state, the total agreement of all with all.

The first public mention of censorship, as we have seen, occurred in July, 1967 when *Literární noviny* printed the resolution of the Fourth Writers' Congress against the wishes of the censors' office. Even this brought reproaches from veteran communists who wondered why the writers were not satisfied with the current practice. 'There are no blank spaces in *Rudé právo* these days! Do you remember what it used to look like sometimes under the pre-war Republic?' If *Literární noviny* had been allowed to exhibit its deletions, those veterans would have been amazed to see how much harder today's censors were working than those of the 'thirties. Another contrast with earlier times was that it was possible then to secure publicity for any text by having it read out in Parliament by a sympathetic deputy; it thus acquired 'parliamentary immunity'. Under the communists, however, this possibility disappeared because the relevant legislation was cancelled. Again, there was no legal recourse against the censorship of the 'fifties and 'sixties as it rested on no legal provisions but simply on the whims of the Party centre and its executive machinery; pre-war censorship, however unjust it may have been, was limited in that its procedures were defined by law.

As a result of various protests against the legal irregularity of the system, the Party centre was finally induced to make an 'improvement' which had the remarkable effect of not only legalising it but also of exacerbating it. A new Press Law was drafted in 1966 and came into effect on January 1, 1967. This law is a scandal in the annals of socialism and demonstrates how low the stalinist model could sink. It gave a legal patent to every arbitrary act, making lawlessness into law. Comparison with the moral perversities of fascism is here perfectly in place and it is only the nominal adherence of the authors of the Press Law to the communist movement, and their non-German racial origin, which forbids a still more drastic comparison.

In legalising censorship the law changed the name of the institution performing it from Main Board of Press Control to Central Publishing Board—a gratuitous effort to avoid calling a spade a spade and jump from one euphemism to another, since the whole system remained just as carefully concealed from the public eye as before. The novelty, however, was that the system now enjoyed a legal basis: the fact that it was still incompatible with the Constitution can scarcely have worried the legislators. If it is progress to render legal what was previously illegal, then the Press Law was a progressive step.

Paragraph 2 of Section 17 read as follows:

The Central Publishing Board will ensure that no material is published in the mass information media which contains facts constituting a state secret, economic secret or public service secret. The Board will suspend the publication or distribution of any material containing such facts.

There can be no objection to a state defending its own interests. But protection of state interests was not the reason for the existence of the vast machinery of censorship, and in fact state interests were in no great danger: broadly interpreted as these interests were, it was quite exceptional for the censor to question any text on the ground that it was hostile to the state or jeopardised its safety. During the whole life of *Literární noviny* there was only one case of the censor taking action under this paragraph, or in the spirit of this paragraph prior to the new law. That case concerned a critical reference to the sale of Czechoslovak arms to Nigeria, whose government was using them to suppress a national liberation movement in the course of a civil war and to massacre that part of the Negro population which defied it. This regrettable fact was no secret outside our country and had been extensively dealt with in the foreign press, which was the source of the material used in the article objected to. Let us concede, however, that our state felt endangered by the publication of this news and considered it a state secret. It was still an affecting experience for us to note the solemnity with which the censor took action in this case and even issued a written confirmation, which we kept in the office as a treasured relic. For it was at least an attempt to define the point at which state secrets required protection, even though the definition was somewhat spoilt by the subsequent publicity given to the matter and the embargo on arms deliveries which followed. The lively traffic between our office and the censor's was in fact not normally related to the paragraph quoted above at all. The reason why the censoring officials were so happy to furnish us with an explanation of their objections in writing was that they sensed in this instance, perhaps, a refreshing gust of legality amidst their normal activity, about whose legal status even they must themselves have had misgivings.

For Paragraph 4 of the same Section 17 reads:

> If the content of any material is in conflict with other interests of society, the Central Publishing Board will bring this to the attention of the editor-in-chief and the publisher.

The law's language is here admirably clear. And what, one asks, might these 'other interests of society' be? Who determines and interprets them? Who insists on their satisfaction?

We had in fact ample evidence every week of the wide meaning attributable to that expressive 'other'. It covered every single topic mentioned in the last chapter, however difficult it might be to demonstrate that any 'interest of society' demanded concealment of the economic and social condition of the country. It was of course only the Party centre's interest which in this way maintained its inviolability and immunity to criticism, and concealed its responsibility for the country's crisis. That the Party centre should then appeal to the concept of 'society's interests' to justify the process of keeping society misinformed might be thought a triumph of sick humour if it had not been so brazenly cynical and had such serious effects.

In addition to failing to mention that the 'interests of society', then, are defined by the censors themselves, the law does not explain what happens *after* any 'conflict' under this paragraph has been notified. The senior editors of *Literární noviny* told the censoring officials on many occasions that they were obliged to them for their observations and would accordingly publish the material in question on their own responsibility. But the effect was merely what could be expected. The instrument of the censor's rule was his stamp and it was this stamp, not the editor's signature, which constituted a permit to print. Without it the printing shop was not allowed to print anything and in such cases nothing got printed.

The apparent lacuna in an otherwise amply prescriptive law is to be explained by the existence of internal Party directives supplementing, and aggravating, the law. Both together made a functional whole which certainly did eliminate the 'irregular' aspect of the earlier procedure. Its critics had received a truly stalinist reward for their pains. It puts the law in no better light to point out that the Party directives had been issued before it passed through Parliament. This fact does, however, throw some light on those officials of the Writers' Union who, without seeking the opinion of the members, worked on the drafting of the law and claimed to believe that it would improve the situation. The parliamentary deputies, again, should have found out what they were really voting for even if the insidious effect of the law was not apparent to them from reading it. Probably they knew all along.

As early as September 1966 the Party Presidium passed a resolution, some of whose provisions dovetail excellently with the Press Law that emerged on the following January 1. The crucial passage is this:

... The editor-in-chief, on receiving a notification from the Central Publishing Board, will on his own authority secure the adjustment or deletion of the material in question and discuss it with the author. If the editor-in-chief is told that a notification has been simultaneously passed to his superior political organ then he is obliged by Party discipline to await, if he still wishes to publish the material, the opinion of that organ and to respect its conclusions. In the case of serious incompatibility of views between the supervising organ and the editor-in-chief, or of disagreement between an editorial board and a publishing organisation, on matters of a politico-ideological nature, the editor-in-chief or publisher is entitled to appeal for an opinion to the ideological department of the appropriate Party organ and, if he disputes its conclusions, to the organ itself.

Clearly, if not very tidily, these provisions filled in the gap in the Press Law before it was even sent to Parliament. There is no suggestion here that the censor's powers are limited to *suspension* of

material containing state, economic and public service secrets—
which would leave him with nothing to do. It is made clear on
the contrary that *notification* of an alleged conflict between the
written word and 'other interests of society' is virtual confiscation,
against which lies only an appeal to Party organs. True, the
directive tries to assign some of the task of decision-making to the
'publishing organisation', which in the case of *Literární noviny*
meant the Writers' Union. But such an organisation is only
empowered to decide negatively; no weight attaches to any
positive opinion it may give. In practice, then, the Union could
only function as a delaying factor pending the return of the case
into those hands for which the final decision was reserved,
namely the organs of the Party centre and its *apparat*. And even if
an editor-in-chief chose to ignore the new Party directive and
appeal to the terms of the law, whose scope had been illegally
limited by that directive, the means were available to turn his
protest into an empty gesture, namely the censor's stamp and
the administrative orders to the printers to print nothing without
that stamp. If it came to court, no editor-in-chief would be
in a better position than any other harmless private person. And
in any case, what court in Czechoslovakia would have decided
against a Party Presidium resolution?

The arch was thus completed with the Central Committee
apparat as its keystone. The role of the *apparat* as arbitrator in
censorship disputes was now formally sanctified; so was the Party
centre's role in the exercise of censorship. A glorious climax indeed
for a movement which won its laurels as the doughty foe of
injustice and convention, the pioneer of new ideas! Here was the
kind of document that marked the consummation:

Memorandum

From: Czechoslovak Writers' Union.
To: Central Publishing Board.
Copies to: 1. Ideological Department of the Czechoslovak
Communist Party's Central Committee—attn.
comrade Hotmar

2. Editorial office of *Literární noviny*—attn. comrade
Hamšík.

Dear comrades! The editors of *Literární noviny* have sent to us as the publishers of that paper an article entitled 'Conversations in America' by Stanislav Budín, which they withdrew from publication on receipt of the Central Publishing Board's opinion that it was undesirable for readers to be acquainted with the views of Senator Mansfield and a group of American journalists on the Middle East, these views being 'in conflict with the opinion of *Rudé právo*'. We have read with care the article by Stanislav Budín, who is a competent communist journalist and publicist, and concur with the editors of *Literární noviny* in thinking that the grounds given for withdrawing it are inadequate. We consider indeed that it is a matter for satisfaction if a prominent Czechoslovak journalist obtains a personal interview with an outstanding American politician who, incidentally, does not hide his critical attitude to official American policy. Moreover Stanislav Budín does not reproduce this politician's views passively, but in the form of a dialogue where he comments upon them and argues with them. Budín's article also contains interesting eye-witness evidence on racial victimisation in the U.S. and on the paradoxical development of this imperialist power, in which vast technical progress on the one hand contrasts with harsh class conflicts and human abasement on the other. We therefore request that the article be released.

With comradely greetings,
Yours . . .
Vlastimil Maršíček,
Secretary of the Central
Committee,
Czechoslovak Writers' Union.
Prague, 16 August 1967

Can it be wondered at if, sooner or later, people found it stupid and intolerable to have to write letters of this kind?

It is an ill wind that blows no good. The censors represented not only their own institution but, above all, the Party centre. So that if, in the end, revolt was inevitable, it was not only the censors against whom the country revolted.

7
Degeneration and collapse

I had many good reasons to realise that being editor-in-chief of *Literární noviny* would not, under these abnormal conditions, be a particularly creative job. I had always tried to avoid entanglement in daily disputes with the executors of the Party centre's will: their intrinsic interest was nil and the only trace they left in the mind was disgust and a certain nervous tension which never gave rise to one useful thought or a single good line of prose. Even when I could not escape this sparring I tried to keep a reserve of time and energy for meditation and writing, aware that a man in our profession cannot beat the other side on their home ground except by using their methods. And if he did play by their rules he would not only lose the game but might well lose face and professional standing into the bargain.

However, after a short stay in the corner room of No. 1, Betlemská Street—traditionally reserved for the editor-in-chief—I had to confess that it was impossible to do any work there at all. It was not just that the building was almost completely eroded by the weather and that whenever it started to rain we had to move the furniture around, fetch buckets and spread plastic sheets everywhere. I did not want to suspect the well-meaning public works department of Prague 1 of joining in the Party centre's campaign against *Literární noviny*, even if at a later stage it positively invited this suspicion. For a few months afterwards, when *Literární noviny* had been placed under the Ministry of Culture and then returned to the Writers' Union, I came back to my old office and stood aghast: highly organised teams of repair men, who for years past had been busy on jobs of higher priority, were already hard at work and the rain was not coming through at all. So having our offices requisitioned for a while wasn't altogether a bad thing, we said to ourselves. But in those earlier days we should have been pleased if our only enemies had been go-slow builders and an inefficient service department. There was always the splendid view: if I raised my eyes from my own desk I could see right across the Vltava river to Prague Castle on its hill.

The people who made work impossible were elsewhere.

Shortly after the Writers' Congress I had a visit from two men who introduced themselves by flashing Security Police cards. They asked me to hand them the manuscript of an interview by A. J. Liehm with Ludvík Vaculík. I was the more surprised since the interview had already been published and there was a much simpler way of getting hold of the text, namely by buying a copy of the twenty-third issue of *Literární noviny* at the nearest bookstand. However, the visitors explained that for purposes of evidence it was necessary to have the actual manuscript; a newspaper wouldn't do. I was not sure whether I was entitled to hand the manuscript over since, according to the house rules, all such material had to be kept in the editorial archives for a certain length of time. But the whole affair seemed so suspicious to me that I was about to consult a lawyer, when one of the men saved me the trouble by producing from his pocket a warrant issued by the Public Prosecutor which authorised him to seize the manuscript if it were not surrendered voluntarily. I now learnt that Vaculík was being investigated on suspicion of committing the criminal offence of defamation of the Republic, under the notorious Law for the Defence of the Republic. If I refused to give my visitors the manuscript I should be impeding the execution of an official act.

At this time Vaculík was the subject of Party proceedings, along with Liehm, Klíma and Kohout. The first three of these culprits, now being called to account for the results of the Writers' Congress, were on the editorial staff of *Literární noviny*. I had accordingly been to see senior officials of the Party's Control and Audit Commission in the Central Committee headquarters to try to clear up any misunderstanding there might have been. It was no use; these officials, concerned as they were with Party discipline, had never asked and would not admit any question about the reasons for conflict between the Party leadership and members of the cultural community. They were convinced *a priori* that the writers were guilty and were only interested in seeking some motive for their error in past history. Since their whole attention was directed elsewhere than at the substance of the dispute they had a strange and highly unreal conception of it. It was a depressing encounter. And when we went on to talk about the Arab–Israeli conflict, which was then a favourite topic of back-stage conversation in Party circles, I had the unpleasant feeling that though we spoke the same language we failed to understand each other at all. We were all members of one party, but so far apart in our thinking that our dialogue had turned into two monologues.

That my friends and colleagues were going to be expelled whatever happened during the 'Party proceedings' was abundantly clear to me. Nothing could stop it and the only question was what I, and many others, would then do whose experiences and opinions were far closer to those of the men being expelled than to those of the men who were expelling them. On whose side were we? And on whose side was the Party?

It was possible to argue on familiar lines, of course, that the Party's evolution was a complex one, that it had often passed through crises in the past—especially in its relationship with the intelligentsia and that one should not draw hasty conclusions from a few extreme occurrences. None of this, however, helped to explain the appalling fact revealed by a visit from two Security men to seize the Liehm-Vaculík manuscript. Party proceedings were one thing, the Security Police were quite another. Had we reverted to the situation of the 'thirties and the 'fifties when differences of opinion ended up as court cases? Have the police begun to intervene in ideological quarrels once more? Not that they ever start such a thing on their own initiative; but once they are involved, as past experience has taught us, they tend to conduct the operation according to their own logic and with their own special verve.

I immediately protested against this action, first to my visitors' superior and then to the head of the Party's Ideological Department. The senior Security officer explained to me courteously that his men had been quite within their rights since they were acting on the Public Prosecutor's instructions. František Havlíček, on the other hand, reacted to my indignation over this spillover of ideological matters into the Security field by confirming that the possibility had indeed been mooted in one department of the Central Committee Secretariat that some of Vaculík's remarks were actionable under the Penal Code. No, the initiative had not come from his own department and indeed he disliked the idea. However, there was nothing for it but to let the Security Police collate their material and wait for the Public Prosecutor's decision. Havlíček omitted to tell me, though I learnt it from other sources, that where the initiative *had* come from was the department run by the notorious Mamula[19], whose writ ran in the army, Security forces and judiciary and who was the personal instrument of Comrade Number One.

It was not to be the last such such visit, nor was Vaculík the only target of Security interest: other editors on our paper came under the magnifying glass too. There were various symptoms by which the progression from classical stalinism to Czech neo-stalinism could be traced. Where in former times people would be arrested at night by armed plain-clothes men, now the Public Prosecutor erected a façade of legality. Where in the past newspapers were closed down by brute force, now some legal justification would be sought so that the same end could be achieved more subtly and inconspicuously. The act of suppression was accompanied, Czech-style, by an effort to construct some sort of political platform around the affair, so as to give it moral respectability and win the support of the naive as well as the corrupt.

This outward humanising of stalinism was not, of course, the result of any intrinsic change but a symptom of growing weakness and a response to its opponents' increasing strength. In a clinch, however, the stalinists will undoubtedly shed all these Czech modifications, show their old police-state fangs—and destroy themselves in the process.

The process runs in a vicious circle. The behaviour of reformed stalinists activates their opponents, whose behaviour in turn radicalises the stalinists, inducing them to throw off the reformist guise and revert to well-tried methods of oppression which provoke still greater resistance, and so forth. Compromise, that typical Czech solution, does not provide an answer to every historic situation. Sooner or later there must be a confrontation to decide who is who, and only when that is established can one start looking for a compromise position—which cannot be reached with stalinists anyway. This clarifying and healthy experience (however painful for many people) cannot be avoided by subtle tactics; it can only be postponed. In Czechoslovakia it proved possible to postpone the confrontation from 1956 right up to the spring of 1968. The intervening years of postponement may have seemed to some like years of modest progress; but against a European background they were years of overall retrogression.

It was not only the shadowy figures of the Security forces who helped to radicalise their opponents. (Indeed, if they had concentrated on tackling the growing problems of ordinary crime they would have won friends everywhere instead of foes.) In the publishing world, the chief credit for making the authorities unpopular and honest work virtually impossible must go to the censors. It was thanks to them that every Wednesday and Thursday before another number of *Literární noviny* was due were days of constant tension and vexation.

On each of those days our driver would take the whole set of page proofs for the next Friday's issue along a familiar route from the printing shop to the censor's office and then back to the editors. Throughout the Wednesday and Thursday the censors would be ringing up to say what they proposed to 'suspend', i.e. to veto: sometimes entire articles, sometimes passages which could only appear with the changes they required. The arguments we had over the telephone with the censors, about the reasons for deletion or the feasibility of proposed re-writes, were hard for anyone but a martyr or a humorist to endure. For the censor's eye invariably lit upon tiny facts and allusions, or isolated remarks, which not even he could describe as anti-socialist, and which were only 'in conflict with other interests of society' in the sense of conflicting with the momentary wishes and fancies of the Party centre. The only constant element in the leaders' caprices was their interest in maintaining themselves in power, and the censor's behaviour gave us many a clue as to what the Party centre conceived itself to be threatened by.

Only after many delays and amendments, for example, were we able to publish B. Peychlová's report on prostitution and

Novomeský's appreciation of Teige, while Čivrný's polemic with the writer Ivan Skála, like Liehm's reviews of the films *Report on the Party and the Guests* (*O slavnosti a o hostech*) and *The Daisies* were not allowed through at all. The piece on prostitution was thought to represent a malicious quest for seamy sides to socialist society, though prostitution is hardly a socialist monopoly; that on Teige was seen as a snide critique of contemporary cultural policy. The battle over Novomeský's article lasted from February to June and even then it was only allowed after changes were made which deserve another look.

One passage of Novomeský's originally ran thus:

Neumann's conception of the new Marxist line culminated in 1936 with his notorious pamphlet against Gide, which it is fair to describe as the Czech ABC of dogmatism; so indeed it was understood during the 'fifties when, together with Štoll's *Thirty Years* . . ., it was the basic textbook on the 'Marxist' interpretation of social life and culture . . .

After the obligatory change this passage read:

Neumann's conception of the new Marxist line culminated in 1936 with his notorious pamphlet against Gide. During the 'fifties *Anti-Gide* was the basic textbook, along with Štoll's *Thirty Years* . . ., on the interpretation of social life and culture.

Novomeský goes on to argue that if it is right to excommunicate Teige and the *avante-garde* of the inter-war years from the socialist community, then by the same token

we must also question the correctness of the Soviet Communist Party's Twentieth Congress and consider its conclusions dubious because it revised and corrected the same mistakes, misjudgements and crimes as were pilloried in *Surrealism Against the Stream* (*Surrealismus proti proudu*) . . .

—pilloried, that is, in a book which was still banned in Czechoslovakia when Novomeský wrote this. This reference had to be altered as follows:

. . . we must also question the correctness of the social process which revised and corrected the mistakes and misjudgements of the period of stalinist deformations.

I have quoted these changes in some detail not to illustrate the odd craftsmanship of the censor but to show how the Marxist left-wing were hounded and gagged, and persecution directed not at the opponents of socialism but at those who preached socialism. This is characteristic of the Party centre's doctrinal concerns at that time. In order to maintain its own position, which relied on a twisted view of socialism, it suppressed socialist thought *par excellence*: after all, only socialist writers contributed to *Literární noviny*. The Left, continually exhausted by wearisome disputes and sterile fights to obtain even the slightest scope for creative work, was naturally hindered in its intellectual development and, driven into a false kind of unity by the need for common defence against the authorities, was unable to achieve any internal differentiation. Willy-nilly, many keen supporters of socialism were thus artificially converted into opponents and the impression was fostered that only a narrow élite, or perhaps only Comrade Number One himself, was truly socialist.

Of course, we did what we could in our office to resist the censor's trespasses. In the final phase, in fact, we used to hold so-called 'Debates with the Censorship' every Wednesday and Thursday. The censoring officials usually adduced some doctrinal point as the reason for their demand, such as that the article in question 'took an insufficiently class-conscious view', failed to stress the Party's leading role enough, or was over-simplified and emphasised one aspect at the expense of some other. We would reply that we were quite happy to accept responsibility for this kind of literary or editorial matter. If we managed to carry our point we would bring down subsequent wrath not only on our own heads, but on the censor's as well. Then our telephone would ring and a reproachful voice would say: 'You've got me into a fine pickle now!'

The more meticulously *Literární noviny* was watched, the more arbitrary were the reasons given for each act of censorship. The passage in question, we were told, conflicted with such-and-such a Party and state resolution; or contradicted the official history of the state and Communist Party, never yet revised; or the particular Central Committee official who would probably pass the piece was away; or simply 'the Ideological Department has told us not to let this sort of material be published'. Or again, as the most practical argument of all: 'You can imagine what a stink there'd be!'

After this sort of exchange the same thought often occurred to me that I had had when the Security men came for the Vaculík script, or when I tried to get sense out of the Control and Audit Commission officials. How strange that the censors should be calling us Comrade this and Comrade that; that we should be members of one and the same political party!

What could have happened to a party that now appointed one group of members to keep watch over another? How could it come about that the Party centre should exercise its leading role against its own members through the machinery of the Ministry of the Interior, though this too (like everything else) was subordinate to that same Party centre? How was it that the will of the Party's leaders was only manifested to us as a system of controls, restraints and frustrations? Or that the censor's staff were praised and trusted while we were suspected, attacked and victimised? Were those men the true communists, perhaps, and the left-wing intellectuals heretics unworthy of the Party? Why was our Party bidding farewell to the foremost writers, philosophers and historians, the cream of both our peoples? Or were only the present leaders of the Party taking this step? Did all these headaches come from a concatenation of practical blunders, or were they symptoms of a wider malaise afflicting the very roots of the socialist movement?

There is no clear answer to all these questions yet. But one thing is clear: the Czech and Slovak intelligentsia displayed in this predicament the sincerity of its faith in a socialist solution for the ills of our society, even though everything had been done for years on end to drive them away from any such belief.

By the summer of 1967 when preparations were being made, in the aftermath of the Writers' Congress, for the long-postponed blow against *Literární noviny*, the censor's pressure had become quite intolerable. It was not unusual for a third of the material prepared for the forthcoming issue to be confiscated. If I had to be away over Wednesday and Thursday, I found myself looking at quite a different paper when I bought it on Friday from the one I had left behind me. Things finally reached the point where our paper was not even allowed to reprint passages of our choice from books or even from other newspapers. This ban fell, for example, on an excerpt from an article in the technical magazine *T 67*, in which an architect discussed planning mistakes made in connection with the construction of the Prague underground railway that had led to a loss, in one instance alone, of some 500,000,000 crowns—the equivalent of at least 6,000 flats at the new prices!

When we protested angrily against interference with material which had already been passed for publication elsewhere we were given various explanations: that what applied to a technical journal might not apply to a literary one; that a book has a small circulation while our paper has a big one; or that specific criticisms acquired a different and undesirable connotation when they appeared in *Literární noviny*.

An historian friend of mine who happened to be present at one of our talks with the censors could not understand how we tolerated it. Furious at what he had witnessed, he told us that whenever the telephone rang and the censor's office came through we should simply tell them to go and chase themselves, or some stronger phrase, and hang up. These humiliating experiences enabled outsiders, amongst other things, to appreciate Vaculík's stand at the Congress. Many had criticised him for using such strong language and inviting retaliation in kind. But once they had a chance to see the censorship machine at work they realised how restrained Vaculík had in fact been.

Literární noviny was not allowed to put out an article by Petr Weiss which was considered by Western critics rabidly pro-socialist, but by our rulers 'anti-socialist'. It was not allowed to publish the text of Deputy Pružinec's question in Parliament (referred to on p. 89), with its demand for the banning of two *nouvelle vague* Czech films, since this would be 'adding fuel to the flames'! An eight-page article about Masaryk by Professor J. L. Fischer back came from the censor with more than half of it cut, the remainder being a summary of hostile opinions; Fischer's own comments on these opinions, and his views on Masaryk himself, though written from a socialist standpoint, were declared unsuitable. The point of the article had by then been completely lost and we decided to scrap it entirely. In this particular case, however, the approval procedure was transferred from the censor's office to the Party Secretariat itself, and we were treated to the spectacle of a frightened woman official, who would scarcely have passed the preliminary test to attend one of the professor's seminars, suggesting to him not merely what he should delete but even what he should add! She wanted him, for example, to improve his closing sentence:

The task before us is to complete the edifice of socialism in accordance with the laws of our nation's life and growth,

by appending the words 'in the spirit of proletarian internationalism'. When we rejected this, amongst other reasons because we were not entitled to insert fresh material into an author's text, she asked that we should put in an asterisk and a footnote supplying 'proletarian internationalism' as an editorial afterthought.

That was really the limit, we thought. But it was becoming clearer every day that the censors were losing sight of the last shreds of their own rickety logic and that their activities were now just a smokescreen behind which the Party centre was preparing to give *Literární noviny*, so long a thorn in its flesh, the final *coup de grâce*.

Two incidents from the last months of the paper's life confirmed what we had gathered from various indiscretions, namely that the decision in favour of the *Endlösung* represented a victory of injured vanity over sober calculation.

The first of these concerns the affair of the so-called 'Czechoslovak Writers' Manifesto'. It later transpired that this none too brilliant text had been written by a none too well-informed historian, Dr Ivan Pfaff, who placed it in the London *Sunday Times* with the help of the émigré agency run by Mr Jan Josten. This otherwise very reliable paper, largely due no doubt to the absence of any genuine news about the Congress, accepted the 'Manifesto' as authentic and released it to the world as a desperate appeal by Czechoslovak writers for assistance against the terror that faced them. As it had been forbidden to publish anything about the Congress in our own press, apart from attacks on 'anti-Party' and 'anti-state' speeches whose content was not revealed at home or abroad, the 'Manifesto' may well have struck the distant British reader as plausible. He was helped to this conclusion by Mr Josten's agency, which misled him in the most essential particular, declaring that the original document bore the signatures of 183 Czech and Slovak writers whose names could not be published for fear of exposing them to still greater persecution.

The 'Manifesto', as often happens when true news is concealed and fertile ground thus prepared for misinformation and provocation, attracted considerable attention throughout Europe. Many prominent writers believed it and felt obliged to show solidarity by writing to the papers. Günther Grass sent an open letter to President Novotný and published it in the press. This development was far from welcome to the Party centre, which had been trying to acquire a progressive image abroad and even at home hoped to show that all the mishaps at the Congress were the fault of a few adventurers, and that their punishment would be welcomed by that healthy core of the literary community which supported *their* sort of socialism. This was why they had banned publication of Congress news, and then spread false stories about it through Party and other channels, finally allowing *Rudé právo* to publish in carefully measured doses its articles denouncing those unknown 'anti-socialist' speeches, as well as a few extracts from these to make the case. The tale was even circulated that the whole Congress had been organised by émigré circles in Paris, showing that the stalinists' technique for manipulating public opinion and stirring up animosity has not developed much originality over the years.

The Party centre would have been highly delighted if the writers themselves had exposed the 'Manifesto' as a forgery and dissociated themselves from it. Nothing would have been easier, of course, than to denounce it through the official C.T.K. agency, but more credence would be given to the unofficial voice of the writers and the writers' own weekly. We even received an offer from the Central Committee *apparat* that we could reprint the 'Manifesto' provided we accompanied it with an editorial denunciation.

It was not clear at first where the 'Manifesto' had come from, but it was clear from internal evidence that it had not come from native literary circles since it was at odds with the spirit and with the practical demands of the Congress, which represented the thinking of the Union and of our paper. The document was a mixture of truth, half-truths and falsehoods such as could only be believed if the true facts were hidden. The alleged numbers of signatures—183—was itself enough to suggest forgery, for this amounted to nearly half the Union's membership and we must needs have known some of the signatories personally.

In view of this the paper's editorial board would have been able quite sincerely to denounce the 'Manifesto' as bogus. But it wished to add that documents of this kind can only arise when there is a lack of true public information, that is, in situations where extremists of both poles tend to use provocation as an instrument for their own ends. In very moderate terms, then, the board would have hinted that the whole stir about the 'Manifesto', and the Congress, might have been very different or perhaps not taken place at all if publication of material from the Congress had been allowed.

Not even this editorial statement, however, was allowed, and therefore we could not print the 'Manifesto' either. The Party centre considered the editors' attitude impudent, though it merely followed the lines of the resolution passed by the Congress as the Union's supreme organ, and *Literární noviny* was under formal obligation to do this anyway. Amidst the angry official reaction to the episode the threat could be heard that the Party centre would soon be able to manage without any statements from our quarter anyway—in other words, it would manufacture them for itself.

The second incident was the departure from the country of the Slovak writer Mňačko,[18] which was instantly denounced as treason. Mňačko was then not only expelled from the Communist Party, but deprived of his civic rights as well. This was a punishment that had never been meted out even to genuine traitors and sworn foes of the Republic who had fought against it in the service of foreign armies. At the same time it was clear from Mňačko's statements and comportment abroad that he was taking care that his critical remarks about the Party leadership were not, and could not be, interpreted as defamation of the Republic. He restricted himself for the most part to criticising the official line on the Arab-Israeli conflict, saying that the impossibility of expressing disagreement with this at home was the reason why he had come abroad to express disagreement with it there. At the same time he pointed out the dangers of anti-semitism, which had played such a baneful role during the political trials of the 'fifties— and at every allusion to the Slánský trial several leading Party members, notably Comrade Number One, reacted with such venom that one could well infer guilty consciences. Mňačko, it should be mentioned, had also had a protracted dispute with various officials over his book *The Taste of Power* (*Jak chutná moc*), whose publication in Czech by the Writers' Union's own publishing house was stopped at the last moment on Novotný's orders.

Our paper never printed official news stories even about literary matters, for one thing because they would already have been used by the radio, television and daily press. We therefore gave no thought to the question of reprinting the C.T.K. communiqué which stamped Mňačko a traitor and announced his loss of Party membership and civic rights. Nor did we consider putting out the statement that shortly followed it from the presidium of the Slovak Writers' Union. This was not because the Slovak statement, albeit in more measured terms, regrettably included judgements on Mňačko's morals and on his ability as a writer—a tactless thing in the circumstances, so much as to say 'Now you've run away we'll halve your marks!' But the statement had already been printed and broadcast; and furthermore it was not usual or obligatory for us to print statements by the Slovak Writers' Union since *Literární noviny*, for all the excellent relations it enjoyed with it, was not that Union's paper. The Czech section of the Czechoslovak Writers' Union had no separate leadership then, and this latter Union was unable to function properly since the Party's Central Committee had prevented it from electing its senior officers and forbidden its committee to convene.* There

* In September 1967, at a subsequent session of the Union's committee, the Mňačko affair was discussed. The committee deplored the fact that he had gone abroad but also protested against the severity and precipitate speed with which he had been stripped of his citizenship. Since, however, permission was given to publish the condemnation but not the protest, the Union's committee forebore to publish the resolution at all and merely communicated its contents in internal letters to the Party's Central Committee and to the Ministry of the Interior.

was no one, then, empowered to make a statement on the Mňačko affair on behalf of the Czechoslovak Writers' Union, and therefore nothing for *Literární noviny* to print. I happened to have occasion around this time to talk to some officials of the Central Committee's Ideological Department on another matter. When I was asked how we proposed to comment on the Mňačko business, I said we should summarise the content of the official announcement and explained why we should not be printing full versions either of that announcement or of the Slovak Union's statement. They thought my answer was understandable in respect of the official report, but asked me to reconsider my intention to ignore the Slovak statement. The whole exchange was very polite and we parted amiably enough.

On the day that *Literární noviny* came out, however, carrying neither the report nor the statement, I happened to meet one of the same officials in a corridor of the Party Secretariat building. This time he was absolutely incensed. The expressions 'pig-headedness', 'playing with fire' and 'deliberate provocation' were among the milder ones that he used to describe our paper's treatment of the Mňačko case. When I reminded him about our recent meeting, which could not have led me to think he attached such earth-shaking importance to the affair, he snapped out: 'Don't try and shift the blame on to us!'

Later I was to learn the reason for this sudden change of front. Fire and brimstone had been raining down on these officials' heads in the meantime from a higher quarter. I was really not so naive as to try and transfer my responsibility to anyone else, but what my interlocutor was afraid of was that I might damage his position by quoting our earlier talk. The Central Committee's Ideological Department was only one cog in the machinery operated by the Party's inner core, and above all by Number One. In that maze of conflicting interests and ambitions, where promotion depended first and foremost on unswerving loyalty to Novotný, the Ideological Department was often the black sheep, accused of inefficiency and equivocation, even of issuing mild remonstrations instead of stern calls to order. Several officials and several heads of the Department had fallen victim to Novotný's displeasure, supplemented by the ambition of harder-hearted comrades from other parts of the *apparat*. There were other departments which organised their work far more efficiently, so that everything followed or even anticipated the wishes of Number One. The Secretariat's vast headquarters was a world of its own, with rules unparalleled elsewhere. But since the whole country was directed, actually or theoretically, from this building, its inhabitants easily succumbed to the notion that conditions inside it were an accurate reflection of those outside. The illusion took root that whatever could be easily ordered or arranged within the headquarters could be equally easily effected in the real world. And in the affair of the writers and their paper, credence was increasingly given, not to officials of the Ideological Department, but to more reliable and forthright men in better command of the available forces, whether of the Party, the Security Police or the armed services. They were closer to Number One, Number One was closer to them. And so, in trying to solve these literary problems, he came to rely more and more on those parts of the *apparat* which had the big battalions under their control.

It must be stressed that by this time the whole question of *Literární noviny* had been blown up far beyond its original dimensions as an irritant. While in the world outside unsolved economic, social, political and moral crises were bringing the country to the point of collapse, inside the Party Secretariat officials persuaded themselves that our paper, which only sought to describe these facts, was in fact the sole obstacle in the way of national salvation. It was accordingly made a priority task to seize or silence this bastion and quite disproportionate energy was devoted to the purpose.

It would be hard to say whether Comrade Number One's own irritable temperament was the more to blame, or the obsequious zeal of his praetorian *apparat*; probably it was the two factors together, each activating the other so that the original problem was expanded into a huge and alarming affair that required instant counter-measures. Each succeeding issue of *Literární noviny* provoked a storm of indignation in the building, with cries of 'How long shall we tolerate these attacks on the Party and foul slanders against our people's honest handiwork?'—even though nothing of the kind had appeared on our pages.

Once more a situation had arisen that favoured eager sycophants and ambitious careerists, of whom no one could claim there was a shortage in our country. It was all too easy to earn one's spurs as a propagandist by joining the hue and cry against *Literární noviny*, to indicate one's fitness for still higher service, to eliminate a rival by timely denunciation—there was always an ear ready-cocked and grateful for the news. Conmen and line-shooters qualified only to sniff out the secret weaknesses of the influential needed no urging to compose resolutions and invectives; however outrageous, they could be sure of finding a buyer when the victim of their polemics was denied any chance of reply. In cynical circles it became standard slang to speak of 'feathering your nest with Literárky'. More than one official today owes his advancement to this kind of activity, and though some who took part in the campaign may have done so out of conviction, they must have realised at least that they were tilting against an opponent condemned virtually to silence.

It is from the dregs of its informer network that the Party apparatus learns what popularity and acclaim awaits the fulfilment of its wrathful purpose. Every tiro in the corridors of power knows how to enlist the backing of the naive, the ignorant, the deceived and humiliated. Yet the Party will feel all the more fortified in its decision if it has attracted enthusiasm throughout the country (especially amongst those who always concur in what the powerful wish and urge them to be still more radical if they will) and if it appears to its originators as something sprung spontaneously from the depths of the people's soul. Are not all the crimes of every dictator in history surrounded in an aura of this kind, and if the will of the people were what rulers claim it to be, would there not be still more executions and still more injustice— save for the despot's well-advertised generosity?

Such thoughts come to mind when one recalls any of the successive scandals woven around *Literární noviny*, including the last one—the Mňačko affair—and the vast wave of 'spontaneous indignation' it released. 'Novotný will never forgive you for this one!' I was told, almost in a whisper, by one clandestine informant. 'Don't you know he can't stand Mňačko because he thinks he was satirising him in that book they banned? Just mention the name in Novotný's family circle and they're all hopping mad! That was a big mistake you made in your paper, not to tear Mňačko to pieces!'

In building up the reputation of our paper none of us had ever thought it useful to listen to backyard tittle-tattle. Perhaps we missed a point there.

'They won't let you get away with this, you know! You've signed your death warrant now!'

Novotný's regime had evidently reached a stage where it was determined to take steps so completely calculated to serve its own interests that in fact they damaged them.

The last text of ours which the censor banned was a typical one. At the Writers' Congress the philosopher Karel Kosík had delivered an outstanding discourse on the unity of reason and conscience, arising from the dilemma that faced Jan Hus at the Council of Constance.

On June 18th, 1415 a great Czech intellectual wrote from his cell: 'A certain theologian has told me that everything will be well for me, everything will be permitted, if only I submit to the Council. And he added, If the Council were to declare that thou hast but one eye, albeit thou hast two, then it would be thy duty to confess to the Council that it is so. And I answered him thus: If the whole world were to confirm it yet I, having the reason that I have, could not admit it without offence to my conscience.'

This text, prepared for inclusion in *Literární noviny* in pursuance of the resolution of the Union's committee, was confiscated by the censor on the ground that, in the present situation, it would be provocative. In vain I urged the Union's provisional leaders to authorise me to reject the censor's decision and to insist on publication of the text to the last. Unstamped, the printers would not be able to print it, and *Literární noviny* would not appear that week. Many times we had been about to take this step, yet in the end we always drew back rather than give grounds for stopping the paper altogether. This time there was nothing left to lose.

A session of the Party's Central Committee had already been convened with the task of approving the Party centre's final decision to silence our paper and rid itself of that irritating instigator of critical thought which caused it such trouble every week and put Comrade Number One in a rage.

It is not for me to say why or in what precise circumstances the Central Committee plenum approved this project. Some of its members later complained that not even they had been properly informed about the actual course of the Writers' Congress, but only had a few chosen texts to judge from, with their accompanying evaluations and proposals. Certainly some members of the plenum were very well informed, and others could have obtained information without difficulty, if they had cared to. I pass over the question why many of them found unthinkable what in democracies is normal, that is, to disagree with their Party leader. (No doubt they were influenced by fear of disunity and of 'open crisis in the Party', that bogey so diligently fostered in stalinist theory and practice.) A final verdict is still awaited on one story, widely circulated, namely that a number of Central Committee members opposed to Novotný, particularly those from Moravia and Slovakia, nevertheless agreed this time to his demands in order to conserve their strength for the later confrontation which toppled him from power.

One way or another, however, the Central Committee of the Czechoslovak Communist Party accepted the Party centre's assessment of the Writers' Congress and approved its conclusions: the few isolated dissenting voices—those of Václav Slavík and František Vodsloň, for example—were ignored. The writers Ivan Klíma, A. J. Liehm and Ludvík Vaculík were by decision of the Central Committee expelled from the Party; Pavel Kohout, at first proposed for expulsion, was instead given a reprimand and warning; Party proceedings were re-instituted against Milan Kundera, who was belatedly identified as one of the doctrinal mainsprings of the Congress; while Jan Procházka, in view of his behaviour at the Congress and his sins before and after, was dropped from the post of candidate member of the Central Committee. The avenging hand struck, and those historians who are interested in the causes of conflicts between Party leaders and left-wing intellectuals, conflicts which have been recurring with cyclic regularity ever since the onset of stalinism in the 'twenties, were given a further chapter to contemplate.

One innovation, however, appeared in the shape of a collective penalty inflicted on the whole intellectual sector of the public. *Literární noviny* was accused of having become the forum of the anti-socialist opposition; despite many warnings it had escaped from the control of the Writers' Union; and accordingly the Central Committee recommended its transfer to the competence of the Ministry of Culture.

This resolution was remarkable in many ways. Opinions differ on what is socialism and anti-socialism, and definitions of 'opposition' vary. The myth of monolithic uniformity is not new in the communist movement: Novotný only held on to a pattern established by Stalin and continued after Stalin's death.

But the claim that *Literární noviny* had escaped from the control of the writers is a lie, and those who drafted the resolution knew it. I have no reason to exaggerate the importance of the Congress or the cohesion of the Union with its heterogeneous composition. The charge was repeated *ad nauseam* that the Congress was organised. One can only reply, Yes, it was: not, however, by intriguers and managers from *Literární noviny*, but by the critical condition of society itself, including that sector of it that the Congress reflected. The authors of that critical condition were no writers, but the Party centre. The writers revolted against it in the only way they could and this was the basis on which their temporary unity arose—a unity in normal times unachievable and undesirable. Paradoxically, they were welded into this unity by the ideas and methods of the Party centre, with which no further compromise was possible. Since the wrongheadedness and immorality of the bureaucratic perversion of socialism were easier to observe in a committed newspaper than at an author's desk, the impulse for the writer's revolt grew naturally around *Literární noviny*, itself a sufferer for years past from the pressures and manipulations of the centre. And since I was only associated with the paper for a short time I may perhaps be allowed to say that the writers' community can be proud to have had a journal of that quality. With all its shortcomings, it enabled the writers to play a role for which it would be hard to find a precedent, a role that finds its place in the best traditions of our nation. The finest aspect of the Fourth Writers' Congress was that the writers were able to stand their ground, say their say and refuse to retreat despite all pressures and enticements and attempts to corrupt them, morally and physically. With very few exceptions they held together as a whole, with their paper, disregarding their natural differences for the time being and so in a sense transcending themselves.

All this was perfectly well known to those who drafted that reference in the Central Committee resolution to our paper 'escaping from the control of the writers.' It expressed not a fact, but a hope that *Literární noviny* would be taken over by less committed writers, willing to make unworthy compromises and collaborate with the Party centre in the way it wished. It was an attempt to set up a new forum in place of the one the Central Committee had just liquidated. And the attempt might have worked if previous interventions had not been so palpably unjust as to deter anyone with a conscience and a face to save from risking collaboration.

It was not, be it noted, decided to return *Literární noviny* to the *writers'* hands, which would have been the logical thing to do if the paper really had 'escaped from their control'. It was decided instead to transfer it to the Ministry of Culture, in other words to place it under the direct care of the Party centre, to serve which the ministry had been created. This trivial lapse of logic augured the Party centre's decline into such a narcissistic condition that it could only harm itself. Perhaps it was just a wrong decision even in terms of the existing system. Perhaps, on the other hand, the Party had little choice left, for its autocratic interests had produced too great a conflict with the interests of those who were led. The centre had to create the illusion that it was leading its subjects in their own name and interest; for otherwise it would have to admit that it had passed from covert to overt dictatorship, so denying its own ideological dogmas on which the whole fragile structure of its despotic rule depended.

The climax of the resolution, however, is the recommendation to transfer *Literární noviny* to the hands of the Ministry of Culture. Here again we see the combination of neo-stalinist technique with Czech sleight of hand. Anyone who reads this sentence and envisages what lies behind it may well sigh with relief. Little Czech Machiavelli saves the day!

The history of stalinism is rich in acts of suppression and veto. In the same professional context one could quote the prominent Polish journal which took the demolition of the stalinist system too literally and had to be silenced lest it stand in the way of that gradual return to a moderate variant of the same thing called the 'Polish long-way-round'. So now we could watch the Czech method of doing what in Poland had been effected by simple proscription.

If he reads of a 'recommendation for transfer' to the Ministry of Culture, the uninitiated observer may suspect nothing worse than a routine reorganisation by which bureaucratic bottoms are reluctantly shifted from one set of office chairs to another. Which was precisely what the phrase was intended to suggest.

On the very day that the resolution was published representatives of the Writers' Union and of *Literární noviny* were summoned to the Ministry of Culture, where a senior official, stony-faced, told them that the paper had been unfaithful to its declared mission and that its routine application for registration would therefore be rejected.

At this point we must revert to the mysteries of the new Press Law of January 1, 1967. Beside altering the censorship arrangements it had also changed the regulations for licensing new periodicals. The new provisions had been advertised as a great improvement, and juridically perhaps they were. The explanatory statement sent to Parliament when the bill was passed had this to say:

> For the establishment of a right to publish, the Law replaces the existing *licensing* system by the more progressive arrangement of *registration*. Provided the conditions cited in the law are met, the appropriate authority is bound to carry out the registration of any new periodical . . .

To comply with the new law all existing periodicals had to submit their registration applications to the Ministry of Culture during the course of 1968. This was widely assumed to be a formality; the Ministry showed no great alacrity in dealing with applications, but periodicals continued to be published and their editors did not bother to make enquiries. Only in the case of *Literární noviny* did the new procedure turn out to have a special point. The introductory part of the registration form provided space for a brief and general description by the publisher of the 'mission' of his paper. It was this declared mission which the official now informed us *Literární noviny* had betrayed and would therefore not be re-registered. Since the whole procedure is treated in the new law as a matter of record-keeping it makes no provision for appeal against a negative decision, the possibility of which is not even envisaged.

The practical effect of this legal *tour de force*, as noted in the record of our visit to the Ministry, was that *Literární noviny* would appear that week for the last time as the Writers' Union journal. The Ministry had forbidden nothing; it had merely omitted to register a paper which had been appearing for fifteen years in an edition numbering hundreds of thousands. But never mind, it was now to appear no longer, and the right of appeal, though granted by our legal system to spies and sex murderers, did not in this case exist. This way, please.

There was a storm of indignation in the offices of the Union and its journal. At first it was thought that the Ministry had acted illegally, but consultation revealed that the step taken was completely in harmony with a law ingeniously adapted to ensure the formal correctness of utterly arbitrary administrative machinations. Ivan Klíma had declared at the Congress that the new law was 'a broom that swept well'. Well, *Literární noviny* had been swept right under the carpet and Klíma had been expelled from the Party for his kindness. True, he had not been dismissed from his job, but instead had been deprived of his employer.

Such, then, are the two sides of the Czech brand of reformed stalinism. The side exposed to the public 'recommends transfer to the competence of the Ministry of Culture' while the other, concealed in office files, prohibits without appeal. The big stick is swathed in legality. A better, gentler way of doing things? Perhaps, but really a more corrupt one.

The official explanation justifying the non-registration of *Literární noviny* for failure to fulfil its declared mission adduces the following reasons.

In publishing information on the Congress the paper did not mention the proposal of the Party Central Committee's Ideological Commission, made by Comrade J. Šotola at the end of his introductory speech, to convene a conference of the Union. (Cf issue No. 26)

The list of newly elected members of the Union's central

committee was divided into Czech and Slovak parts, contrary
to the spirit of the Union's Statutes. (Cf issue No. 27)

No publicity at all was given to the protest resolution at the
Writers' Congress against events in Vietnam, Greece and the
Middle East.

The paper had adopted no fundamental stand regarding the
activities of L. Mňačko. It merely issued an 11-line factual story
in its issue No. 33. It did not even put out the statement of
the presidium of the Slovak Writers' Union.

Similarly the paper failed to deal essentially with the so-
called Czechoslovak Writers' Manifesto apart from the brief
démenti put out by the secretariat of the Czechoslovak Writers'
Union and a single sentence in the communiqué on the meeting
of the Union's central committee, in issue No. 37.

The paper's editorial board made a politically immature
decision when, in protest against a recommendation not to
publish anti-state and anti-Party speeches made at the Fourth
Writers' Congress, it decided not to reproduce any of the
Congress discussion at all.

Issued this 26 September 1967

At the end of this masterpiece, evidently composed by an
official either of the Ministry of Culture or of the Party Central
Committee *apparat*, was appended a review of the paper's past
activities which undoubtedly had its origin somewhere in the
censorship machinery.

During the period between the Third and Fourth Congress of
the Czechoslovak Journalists' Union the staff of the Central
Publishing Board intervened in the work of *Literární noviny* on a
total of 381 occasions. In every case action was taken because of
a conflict between material submitted and other interests of
society; in no single case* was it taken in defence of a state,
economic or public service secret.

The breakdown of the total number of interventions, year
by year, is as follows:

* A slight editorial error: there was *one* such case, *vide* p. 113 (D.H.)

1963 25 interventions
1964 124 interventions
1965 85 interventions
1966 57 interventions
1967 (up to September 23)
141 interventions

Thematically the interventions covered a wide range of issues, from attacks on the Party and state system, and rejection of the Party's leading role in culture and art, to economic and social questions. A number of interventions concerned incorrect understanding of the struggle against deformations in the cultural or political life of the state that had arisen during the so-called period of the personality cult.

No one will be so simple-minded as to assume that the Party's Central Committee had made harmless recommendations which the wicked Ministry of Culture then acted upon with excessive rigour. Every measure taken against the Writers' Union and its paper was conceived in the mind of the Party centre; by the time the Party's Central Committee was approving its proposal for the transfer of *Literární noviny* to the Ministry of Culture an entire executive *apparat*, including Ministry officials, was ready to implement the takeover according to a schedule designed to make it look like a rescue operation.

The plan in no way presupposed that the paper would cease to appear. Then everyone would realise it had actually been banned and the whole camouflage effort, with its legal explanations and declarations of the Party's confidence in the creative writers and its talk of a 'healthy core' in the literary community, would have been in vain. On the very same day I learnt from officials of the Central Committee *apparat* that *Literární noviny* would go on being published, but with a different organisation behind it than the Writers' Union and from a different publishing house than the Union's Československý spisovatel. Who was going to make the real decisions, however, emerged when one of these officials invited me to continue working on the paper, not as editor-in-chief but in some other senior capacity.

'And wouldn't this,' I asked, 'require the approval of the Party's Central Committee organs, which have already refused to confirm me as editor-in-chief?'

'Oh, this would be quite different.'

I was in some difficulty how to react to the offer. When, however, on the following day Jan Zelenka,[20] already installed as editor-in-chief of the new ministerial *Literární noviny*, tried to persuade me to act as his deputy for three months or so and then go off to write on my own, or do a world tour, I didn't think it necessary to tell him my real feelings. The idea of being Zelenka's deputy under any circumstances, let alone under those we were faced with, struck me as highly grotesque. I had not originally wanted to take the *Literární noviny* assignment and when I finally did so it was to give the paper and the Union some kind of help at a time when they needed it, and because I enjoyed the prospect of working with Klíma, Vaculík, Kliment, Liehm, Pochop and other friends and kindred spirits. With Zelenka I could easily have had a row on the spot. However, it occurred to me that the decision to wind up '*Literárky*', as it was affectionately called, would bear particularly hard on some of the older staff who had come to us from its predecessor *Lidové noviny*, devoted the best years, or practically all the years, of their life to the paper and might now find themselves out on the street with two years to go till their pensions. I felt it was my duty to secure them the chance of staying on if they wished under the new management, if only for long enough to see how things settled down or look around for alternative work: for their financial prospects were grim indeed. So when Zelenka hinted that my going into his paper would make it easier for other editors to be transferred too, and that I could make this a condition, I made my mind up.

'Right, I'll stay on condition that Klíma and Vaculík and Liehm all stay too.'

And so we parted. But how little I really knew those senior colleagues of mine! When the editorial board met for the last time and we told them about the offer for them to stay on, and for Jungmann, too, who was very close to them, and went on to plead with them to remember their families rather than make heroic gestures, and assured them no one would think ill of them for remaining, they did not hesitate for a moment. Years of exposure on that high-risk job had prepared them so perfectly for the crisis that they rejected the offer to a man. It was a moment I shall never forget. We on the editorial board were all in a safer financial position and knew we could find other employment more easily than the staff editors, men entirely absorbed in the day-to-day labour of bringing out a particular paper, labour often deadly dull, petty and inconspicuous, on whose conscientious performance the visible impact of the finished product was nevertheless utterly dependent. For us, it was merely a moral imperative that we should have nothing to do with the new firm. For them, there was a serious threat to their livelihood, something which in our part of the world normally dampens any enthusiasm for justice. (At least one historian has seen economic hardship as the prime root of Czech opportunism; the Czech 'little man' does not exactly sell his ideals, but trades them for the necessities of life.)

We had mixed feelings as we cleared out the ramshackle editorial rooms at No. 1, Betlemská Street where we had spent so many good times and bad times together, and which we now had to vacate at twenty-four hours' notice. Colleagues and contributors came to say goodbye to us, and so did the postmen with their express letters, still hoping to catch us at the old address.

Dear friends,

It's just gone six in the morning on Thursday, 28 September, 1967 and I've got a strange tense feeling in the pit of my stomach. I was listening to the news. I know you've got plenty of troubles of your own just now, but I'd like to share mine with you as well. How is it possible that anyone can rob the Czechoslovak Writers' Union of their own weekly paper? Everyone knows that the old *Literárky* hasn't 'escaped from the writers' control'. Everyone knows that its readers stand by it and love it! It's hard to have to write this, But I don't believe yesterday's decision by the Party's Central Committee about handing over the paper to the Ministry of Culture was a proof of strength, really. It was something I don't like the sound of. You can never win the battle for truth by throwing your weight around. But don't be downhearted, dear friends. Your readers are behind you. If you should happen to put out another paper, even a cyclostyled one, do please send it to me.

Miroslav Frydrych,
Bohuslavice,
Náchod district

Many visitors came to our door—well known, less known and completely unknown. At one moment when I was sitting in a room alone with Ludvík Veselý, doing something urgent and not wanting to be disturbed, four young lads forced their way in and pressed us to accept some money they had collected in their home district. An old woman from Chomutov, who had been sending Vaculík twenty-five crowns every fortnight since the Congress, and apologising that it couldn't be more (she never enclosed her address so that we couldn't return her the money or even thank her for it), turned up to ask what address she should send her contribution to now. A letter came from editors of the literary monthly *Host do domu* in Brno.

Dear colleague,

Since *Literární noviny* has ceased to exist in its traditional form we hereby put at your disposal the pages of *Host do domu*, which is still an organ of the Writers' Union. It will probably involve difficulties, but we should be pleased to see your writing in our magazine. Please do not think we are trying to profit from the situation in which *Lidové noviny* and its staff find themselves; we would just like you to feel that *Host do domu* is a forum where you can go on doing useful work even in trying times.

On behalf of all the staff,
Jan Skácel, Editor-in-chief

8
Mamula calls in the army

Meanwhile, in another place, a fresh team of editors for the ministerial *Literární noviny* was being put together. I had no inside knowledge of what was happening, but Czechoslovakia is a small place and everyone knows everyone else, so I could get a pretty good idea from the titbits I picked up. One day I had a telephone call from Colonel Vladimír Diviš, whom I had known from working with him on the army magazine *A-revue*, of which he was editor-in-chief. He made no secret of his ambition to take on a bigger paper some time—a Czech equivalent of the West German *Spiegel* tabloid, for example. His voice sounded very excited.

'Hey, I say, shall I take over *Literárky* as editor-in-chief? What do you think, yes or no?'

What could I say but that it was up to him, and if he wanted to know how *I* felt about it, perhaps he had been told that I wasn't on the paper and wouldn't be from now on?

'They called me in to Hendrych's office this morning,' he went on, 'and now they're making it an order: I've *got* to do it!'

I wasn't quite sure how a colonel ought to react to an order of this sort, but it was strange to hear of Hendrych in this military role.

'You know how it is. The Main Political Board hands out an instruction and that's that.'

After talking for two hours with the then head of the Central Committee's Press Department, Miroslav Karný, Diviš had still held out and despite all persuasion stuck to his decision not to join *Literární noviny*. But the rest of the story was later reconstructed by Jaroslav Kokoška in a documentary series published in *A-revue*.

First thing in the morning Lieutenant Colonel Hůrka, head of the Press Unit in the Main Political Board, asked the O.C. of the Board to stop Diviš from being transferred to *Literární noviny*. He pointed out that it was quite improper to 'poach' people from military editorial posts . . . However, requests had come from the Secretariat of the Party's Central Committee not only for Diviš but for other people too. So discussion started in the Press Unit to see what journalists, assuming they were willing, could be spared for *Literární noviny* . . . On the same day, Monday, Lieutenant Colonel Hůrka and the C.O.'s adjutant Major General Gros were called to the Secretariat. First they saw Colonel Švagera on the staff of the 8th Department and then the Press Department head, Karný. Let Lieutenant Colonel Hůrka now take up the story: . . . They first told us that this was a Party assignment that couldn't be turned down. But Comrade Gros objected to this formulation on principle. They still wanted Diviš to transfer to *Literární noviny* right away. We wouldn't have this. We said they'd have to talk to the individuals themselves; *we* couldn't direct them into work like that and it wasn't a matter for the Main Political Board anyway. They kept on trying to convince us that it was our job to persuade Diviš and the others to switch over. At that point Sekera, the deputy head of the Central Committee's Ideological Department, said something that made us laugh. 'You still give orders in the army, don't you?' It was so naive we didn't even bother to react. But then Karný made a statement that had us pricking our ears up. 'We have permission to ignore all the norms.'* I realised then that we were skating on thin ice; the matter had already been settled and it didn't make any difference whether we gave our agreement or not. So after

* Miroslav Karný has explained this as follows. '. . . It was one of the rules of the "nomenklatura" that appointments to certain functions were decided by the Secretariat of the Party Central Committee But after making its decision about the fate of *Literární noviny* the Secretariat transferred this authority to Comrades Hendrych and Havlíček. What I meant in connection with Comrade Diviš—who was Chief Army Editor and so on the Secretariat's register—was that he could be transferred to the *Literární noviny* post without sticking to the normal nomination procedure.

some more pressure General Gros and I made a compromise: if our chaps were willing they could transfer to *Literární noviny* for three months and then come back to the army. But the Comrades in the Central Committee would have to deal with them direct about the transfer question . . .

On Tuesday morning Colonel Diviš turned up at the Main Political Board. Hůrka and Gros met him with long faces. 'We're afraid there's nothing we can do about it, Vladimír. You'll have to go there for the three months, anyway.'

An hour later a group of people were sitting in the office of the head of the Central Committee's 8th Department: Miroslav Mamula himself, his subordinates General Gomulka and Colonel Švagera, Lieutenant Colonel Hůrka for the Army's Main Political Board, and Diviš.

Vladimir Diviš repeated his arguments. He was now sitting for the first time in his life opposite Mamula, a man he had often heard about but never met face to face. He knew he was not in Mamula's good books. He had heard rumours several times that Mamula wanted him out of the army because of his class origin. Now this very man was looking sternly into his eyes, and Diviš had an uncomfortable feeling that Mamula could read his thoughts.

'You must realise, Comrade Mamula, that as an officer I can't take over a job like that. Imagine if someone says "You may be a colonel and you can order people about in the army, but not in a newspaper office!"'

'If someone says that to you, you sock him on the jaw.'

What came after that was just a formality. The whole bunch of them trooped off to Karný's office next. By then they weren't concerned with Diviš any more but with other candidates for transfer to *Literární noviny*—S. Buchlák from *Obrana lidu*, who was to start in a week's time, and also L. Tunys from Česko-slovensky voják, but he wasn't to be persuaded and turned the job down. . . .

(From *A-revue* 11/1968)

It seems absurd that the continued publication of *Literární noviny* should have to be ensured by the army and that appointments of editors should be dealt with not only by the Ideological

Department of the Central Committee but also by the Eighth, i.e.
military and security, Department including its head, Miroslav
Mamula, *éminence grise* and right-hand man of Antonín Novotný.
People now had to be pressured, and even ordered, to become
editors of a paper which it had previously been considered an
honour to work for, and this at a time when there was a shortage of
editorial posts and many highly qualified journalists were out of a
job! The Party centre was at this stage already conceiving its
interests so narrowly that it had difficulty in finding men to do its
work even from among its most zealous supporters, and had to
make do with whoever was willing.

I cannot say what range of arguments were deployed at this
particular moment by the men in the *apparat* who had to try and
ensure that our former paper continued to appear. I can only report
what their later emissaries from Party and ministerial quarters
used to say as they went round from one writer to another with
the standard bottle of cognac (paid for by the workers, as they say),
trying to persuade them either to join the editorial staff of *Literární
noviny* or at least to write something for the paper. What they
promised to begin with is less interesting than what they ended up
threatening. Getting *Literární noviny* published, they would say, is
the Party's top priority task at the moment and presents everyone
with an opportunity to show their loyalty, just as in February 1948
or during the currency reform of 1953. Whoever fails now is
stabbing the Party in the back and must expect reprisals. Those
who refuse to contribute to the paper must never expect to publish
a line of their own work again, either in periodicals or books.

'And you imagine,' they would sneer, 'that the public will miss
Kundera, Klíma, Vaculík or Procházka? They won't even notice
they've gone. And they won't notice you either, as long as they
get their beer and sausages!' (They had accused the Kunderas
and Klímas of 'insulting the people'. Some of their own sayings
would have made odd mottoes for the new *Literárni noviny*,
however.)

One line of talk that I heard from a Ministry of Culture official
was that there would be no arrests or trials this time—which
made me happy for Vaculík's sake—because such things produced
bogus heroes. We have learnt our lesson, the line went on, and
now we have more effective instruments for controlling people:

the Czechoslovak crown ('Remember how persuasive the zloty and the rouble were?') and, in extreme cases, the lunatic asylum. These thoughts were no less credible for being most openly expressed as I plied the visitors with my own (French) cognac. On whose orders, I wondered, were the accounts opened which made possible largesse on a scale to dwarf any proffered cognac? Who was it that authorised promises, and in some cases disbursements, of sums equivalent to several months of a worker's wages?

In the overwhelming majority of cases, however, these strange requisitioning officers went away empty-handed. If their hosts were mild they made excuses, if they were short-tempered they threw them out—no self-respecting writer allowed himself to be bought, tricked or intimidated. Their first delight at procuring an article from Jiří Šotola turned into something unprintable when they found out that, after much persuasion, Šotola had given them a manuscript only recently banned in the original *Literární noviny*. The ban had to be cancelled so that it could now be printed.

The purpose of all this effort was, of course, to show that the paper had only been transferred, not stopped, and had thus reverted to the original 'mission' it was said to have betrayed. The public were not told that the Ministry of Culture had refused to grant registration to the Writers' Union (and had then promptly registered the paper on the Ministry's own account). The paper continued to appear, though with quite different editors and contributors. There was the same title, the same layout and typography, and the old cartoons were imitated. Although it was really a new periodical its first issue was not called Number 1, Year I but Number 40, Year XVI. Even this was in harmony with the law—one of those egregious laws of ours which allows a huge fraud to be perpetrated on the public in order to preserve an effect of bogus continuity.

This kind of insolence upset the public even more than an open ban on the paper would have done. At a meeting of communist writers shortly after the Central Committee had decided on the transfer, Jiří Hendrych argued in support of the resolution and went into the current policies of the Party leadership at some length. With a victor's self-confidence he claimed that, though the transfer was not something to be pleased about, it had been necessary because the paper had gradually abandoned its function as an organ of the Union and been taken over by a group of publicists whose mixed entourage included even anti-socialist elements. Hendrych also reverted to old complaints: one could make a list, he said, of people whom *Literární noviny* had boosted and launched on successful careers, and another list of names it had blasted and sought to erase from the annals of literature. But the new controllers were trying to restore the paper's original purpose. It would be good, then, if most of the editors were active writers, in fact the Union ought to nominate men for the job.

To the mind of the Party centre this was a pretty eloquent incitement to cooperation. Hendrych went on to mention symptoms of initial reluctance to work along with the new management —he called this an organised boycott—but said he was sure that that reason would triumph.

Had Hendrych himself fallen for all the gossipy slanders and denunciation that his subordinates fed him with as the Party centre wished? It was hard to credit, but his evident surprise at the subsequent course of this meeting suggests that, to a certain extent, he had.

Pavel Kohout now rose to denounce the Central Committee's plenary session for 'disinforming' the Party and the public, and protested against the atmosphere of hysterical suspicion engendered at it. It was easier, he argued, to liquidate a non-existent conspiracy than to analyse why a large number of people had independently arrived at similar conclusions—as the Congress had shown. He asked that the Central Committee should acknowledge its mistakes, since unacknowledged mistakes did nothing to enhance the Party's authority. And he demanded that the Central Committee should give a proper hearing to him, and those like him, who were already half-expelled from the Party.

I watched Hendrych's face. He was controlling himself only by an enormous effort of will.

Some writers spoke up for *Literární noviny* at this meeting who were not associated with it at all and should therefore have been amongst those whom the paper hoped to 'erase from the annals of literature'. Ivan Kubíček of Ostrava, for example, had never written a line for us. Now, he declared that the paper's role had extended far beyond the literary community and that this public prestige was evidently the reason why it had been suppressed. He asked bitterly why there were no penalties for sterility and mental conservatism and suggested that editors who filled their papers with dogmatism should be the ones to have them taken out of their hands.

A broadly based critique of the Party centre's policies came from Professor Eduard Goldstücker, who described the last Central Committee plenum as a step backward in that it restricted freedom, whereas a revolution should be followed by an access of freedom or its whole purpose would be frustrated. This was particularly sour medicine for Hendrych, for Goldstücker was a spokesman of those faithful veterans of the Party on whose support he counted even in his dealings with the other leaders. One of the younger communists who spoke up now was Vladimír Körner, who took up the cudgels in favour of the men recently expelled from the Party and went on very logically to ask aloud whether he should remain a member himself. Antonín Brousek put the same question.

So Hendrych and the whole policy of the Party centre received a mighty and scornful rebuff. Whereas at the start of the meeting he had spoken with the enthusiasm of a political leader successfully putting across his own convictions, his final words were limp and dejected. The resolution was binding on all communists, so they must work on the lines it laid down. Soon we should all see that the Central Committee's measures were wise and would benefit literature by saving it from falling into error.

This said, Hendrych took up his brief-case and left without exchanging a word with anyone. It was the first opportunity he had to meet writers since the Congress, and he was already on his way again.

An equally sharp reaction against the victimisation of the writers and their journal came from the Slovak literary world, whose cautious attitude at the Fourth Congress had encouraged the Party centre to hope it could be exploited, and caused the leaders to smile unwontedly in the direction of Slovakia. At the analogous *aktif* of communist writers in Bratislava a remarkable discourse came from Zora Jesenská, who exposed the fraudulence of the 'transfer' of *Literární noviny* as disguise for a ban which had no justification beyond the narrow self-interest of a Party group engaged in usurping absolute power. She expressed solidarity with her expelled colleagues, finding their speeches anything but anti-socialist. And she ended with this: 'As regards Ludvík Vaculík, I can only say that it is his speech I have thought about most during the past months, and I must admit there were moments when I told myself he had oversimplified some things, put some issues in too absolute terms, judged some phenomena too much in isolation. But my doubts are now dispelled. For the sum of the measures now taken against the writers and their press shows, I regret, that Vaculík's analysis was right.'

Another Slovak, Michal Chorvát, came out against the notion of an 'opposition platform' and protested against the constraints on criticism and creative thought. Jan Kalina made sport of the counterfeit *Literární noviny*, suggesting that it would be almost as impressive if cars labelled 'Rolls-Royce' were turned out in Mladá Boleslav, or Vojtech Cach put Shakespeare's signature at the end of his plays. Samo Falt'an inveighed against the suppression of reports on the Congress; Pavol Števček broke a lance for *Literární noviny* and also repudiated the official bouquets for Slovak 'reasonableness'—an optical illusion, he said, that quite falsified their writers' feelings. Ivan Kusý spoke on similar lines. And Laco Novomeský decried the Central Committee's measures as wrong and harmful for the Slovak, as well as the Czechoslovak, Communist Party, and indeed for the whole communist movement. Finally, the Slovak writers passed a resolution demanding that the Czechoslovak Writers' Union be enabled to issue its own journal again as soon as possible.

Even the wider public, however, much exposed to official propaganda, could not long remain ignorant of the real nature of what had been done. The first chorus of Party applause for the expulsion of the writers and the hamstringing of *Literární noviny* soon gave way to wry grimaces. Plenty of approving resolutions continued to flow into the Central Committee's Secretariat, but even there it was perhaps realised that these proved only how well the machinery was working. Where the authors of 'positive' messages added anything original to the standard wording, they added up to a sad picture. I recently had occasion to look at some of this correspondence in the Central Committee archives and could not help noting the similarity to letters dating from the

German occupation and the time of reprisals after the assassination of Heydrich, letters later collected by the Ministry of the Interior. How many were the creations of wronged and humiliated souls, seeing an outlet at last for their fanatical hatred and so absorbed in themselves as to lose all sense of proportion, demanding an extra penalty here and a fiercer vengeance there, handing their neighbours over to the police and itching to requisition property and see the 'guilty' tortured! If it were only the dregs of society—for every society has those. But what is worse is when the mentality of the dregs is elevated to an average and the abnormal is reckoned normal. Unhappy the government which must cope with fascist moods; unhappy the nation whose government does not shield it from such maladies when they run riot!

Yet even amongst correspondence like this one finds many a warning note, a protest, a plea for explanation and even for rectification of wrongs done. The Czech public still exhibits reflexes inherited from the days of Austrian domination, from the war-time Protectorate and from the tensest years of stalinism: it can read between the lines, judge the unspoken word as well as the spoken and listen to the silent as closely as to the talkative. In the public reading rooms one could still find, if there were nothing better, the ministerial version of *Literární noviny*, almost unchanged in outward appearance though vastly different in tone, standard and content. After the alleged attempt to steal it away, *Literární noviny* had been 'handed back to the writers', had it not? Where, then, were the writers' contributions? Where were the names of authors with whom the reader may often have disagreed, but whose opinions he always found interesting? Why were those men of letters silent, whose names had appeared so frequently in the old days?

After a few numbers of *Literární noviny* had appeared under the new management there was no mistaking the contemptuous wall of silence that had grown up around it. Those 'guardians of progress' who had seen the chance of a lifetime in contributing to the transformed paper found themselves forced to write more and more, so that their names, hitherto little known, became a byword for sycophancy. The vision of a place in the sun soon turned into a penance, dragged out with each succeeding issue into a masochistic exhibition.

Jan Zelenka, who had entered the pages of the ministerial paper with a jovial smile and confident matador's panache now tried to behave as if the whole episode were a misunderstanding. In a debate at the Philosophical Faculty of Prague University he spoke of a talk he had had with Milan Kundera which showed (he declared) that that novelist was well on the road to seeing his mistakes. I remember how offended Kundera was, and infuriated too, so that his mind ran to all kinds of horrible revenge. Finally he wrote a letter of grandiose malice (the deliberate misspelling of the addressee's name is a small detail) and sent it both to Zelenka and to those who had organised the debate.

> You stopped me recently on the street, comrade Zelinka, and we talked for some three minutes. I now learn that in front of a large gathering of students of the faculties of law, philosophy and journalism you made use of my name, called me familiarly by my first name (though we have only spoken together twice) and stated that I now regret the views I formulated at the Writers' Congress and am well on the road to recognising my errors. I shall not consider why you fathered this self-criticism on me. But to avoid repetition I must tell you that I have no reason to change a word of what I said at the Congress, that I do not agree and have never agreed with the measures taken against *Literární noviny* (as I have stated publicly), that I regard your role in this matter as a dismal one and your own performance in that role as grotesque. Please take this into consideration next time you propose to paraphrase any opinion of mine. Greetings, Milan Kundera.
>
> P.S.   I am sure you will not mind my showing this letter to those in whose presence you discussed me.

This letter, like many documents from the Congress, including particularly Vaculík's speech, was copied and distributed from hand to hand throughout the country so that in the end it became known to more readers than if it had appeared in *Rudé právo*. Jan Zelenka stopped writing for *Literární noviny* and after three months quietly withdrew from the paper whose editorial body he had joined with such fanfares.

But what in the last resort do they matter—Jan Zelenka and his friends, who allowed themselves to be enticed on to a stolen paper and found their work go so quickly sour on them? The whole brief and inglorious episode of the ministerial *Literární noviny* only illustrates how obstinately the Party centre persisted in harming itself in the very act of promoting what it took to be its interests. It also testifies to the wide gulf that has grown between these interests and those of the people in whose name it has ruled. When that gulf is not only real, but widely perceived, the crisis of stalinism is at hand. What solutions then occur to the leaders, but to retreat, sacrifice someone here and improve wages there, try and create a new set of illusions—or resort to the big stick. In dealing with *Literární noviny* they combined all these techniques, and showed how limited their utility was. For every week a new number would appear to provide the public with fresh evidence of the very crisis its appearance was meant to conceal, and accelerate the impending fall of the leaders themselves.

The reader might think these assertions exaggerated if the case of *Literární noviny* had remained isolated. But the slow story of its suppression runs in parallel with the ripening crisis of latter-day stalinism. The historian who records the gradual breakdown of stalinist socialism in Czechoslovakia may regard it as a coincidence, such as history loves, that the events concerning the Writers' Congress and the writers' paper coincided in time with two other sets of events—the Slovak revolt and the Strahov incident. Perhaps one may be allowed to remind such an historian of the philosopher's axiom, that coincidence is but a form of necessity.

For many reasons, including the psychology of tyrants, other chronic sources of tension were also approaching the breaking-point. One was the unequal position of the Slovak people, smaller and always relegated to the indignity of second place, its self-confidence and self-awareness snubbed by the Košice Programme, by both subsequent Constitutions and above all by Novotný's despotic theory and practice with its relentless trend to absolute centralisation. For all the smokescreens, his was a system of one master, and that one master in Prague, a man whose domineering behaviour could not but show itself as the assertion of the Czech nation in relation to the Slovak nation, smaller and lagging behind it. For the existence of dangerous nationalistic tensions in our country we must blame not only Novotný's policies themselves, but also the fact that we tolerated him for so long in the leadership as a *Czech* politician and were so blind to the response his power provoked in Slovakia. Into that permanently explosive situation came Novotný, behaving as arrogantly as at home in Prague, insulting the Matica slovenská, that symbol of national advancement, returning gifts sent to him as a goodwill gesture with the insulting message: ADDRESSEE DOES NOT ACCEPT. His remark to his wife at a welcoming ceremony at the Matica slovenská— 'Don't touch anything, Božka, and let's get away!'—was carried swiftly over the length and breadth of Slovakia. It became not just a verdict in itself on the human stature of the autocrat, but the source of a rapid rise of national antagonism, bringing all Slovakia's political representatives at one go into the ranks of Novotný's foes. And though the man who rules this country can do without the writers and do without *Literární noviny*, do without Slovakia he cannot.

With the students likewise, Novotný's regime, notorious for its condescension toward all intellectuals, lived on terms of constant uneasiness, occasionally flaring up as at the Majales procession.[21] What was new about the Strahov affair was not the discontent of the students but the brutality with which its signs were stamped upon—a brutality sparked off perhaps by fears that the marchers were aiming for the nearby Castle of Prague.

All the signs showed that the stalinist system in our country was degenerating rapidly into an unchecked personal tyranny, in which Novotný's growing nervousness would drive him to suppress everything incompatible with his rule, whether it were socialist in spirit or not. Is it insignificant that when, against the background of Central Committee sessions between October 1967 and January 1968, the stories of imperialist plots were resurrected, the targets of those plotters were said to be 'Czechoslovak socialism, the Party, the Central Committee and Comrade Novotný'—as if the whole quartet were really one? Or that Miroslav Mamula was for ever gathering information about enemy intelligence operations, designed to overthrow—Comrade Novotný? And what of the continuous marshalling of army, Security forces and militia to fight the internal foes and frustrate the opposition within the Party and Central Committee to—

Novotný? The outcome of the January 1968 session of the Central mission which ended Novotný's rule was also, in a sense, coincidental, albeit necessary.

When the Czechoslovak spring came round in 1968 the Writers' Union once more applied to register *Literární noviny*. And this time the application was refused because a periodical of that name already existed. And the man in the same office who later told me of the compromise agreed on, namely that the Union's paper could be called *Literární*, but then *listy* instead of *noviny*, and beamed and added his congratulations, was the same Ministry of Culture official who, stony-faced the previous autumn, had notified me that our paper was to be stopped.

It was a stirring moment and I could not resist a dig at him.

'I trust that next autumn you will be here to tell us we are closing down again.'

It was naughty of me, I admit, but in the general optimism it passed unnoticed.

And if anyone finds that too anxious a note to end on, let him wait at least till the autumn.

Postscript

The last few words of this book are referred to by the reading public in Prague as 'that famous sentence'. Authors do not always manage to get their prophecies quite right. But we all know what that 'autumn' brought: the arrival of the five Warsaw Pact armies, putting the seal to Czechoslovakia's spring before any of its blossoms could bear fruit.

In Europe's already troubled sky this military operation traced another angry question mark or, as it seemed to many eyes, exclamation mark. It had the effect—certainly unintended by its planners—of stressing the universal aspect of the Czechoslovak spring, the human content and importance of this still unfinished experiment, even if their propagandists sought to persuade the public of the contrary by calling it a 'purely internal concern' of that socialist world which, in the European context, is also a power bloc and a politico-military structure. It was a concern so purely 'internal' as to send shivers down the spine of a world now forced to realise, once more, upon what fragile foundations its equilibrium rests and how easily crossed is the narrow line that all of us must tread between life and death. This basic and distressing insight makes us look searchingly again at the real aspirations of the spring and ask more sternly than before: Was the experiment worth while? Was it not from start to finish a masochistic exercise or romantic gesture, pre-destined to end the way it did? Did it not put in needless, futile jeopardy the whole world, incuding our beloved Europe and indeed the two nations of Czechoslovakia, themselves? Did its intrinsic worth outweigh the risk that was and still is, bound up with it? Did it contribute something fresh to the pool of human ideals and values from which the civilised world draws spiritual nourishment in its onward journey? Did it at least improve conditions of life in the country that gave birth to it?

It is too early to look for definitive answers. History is not straight and simple; the twists and turns along the circuitous route by which one event follows another forbid us to draw a 'final' conclusion from the aggregate of causes and consequences, circumstances and interconnections. Provisional answers, on the other hand, can be attempted by reconstructing and analysing the Czechoslovak spring as a single season which could still, possibly, become something more.

In this respect the British reader might feel that the book ends where it should begin, with that blossoming of early 1968. But the spring did not arrive unheralded. Such a protracted winter had gone before it that when the thaw started, fast and sudden, its effect was almost explosive. For the reader not closely familiar with Czechoslovak affairs or the general domestic problems of the socialist world, this book may shed light on the way things matured, on the depth of the crisis; it may bear witness that the eventual catharsis was not only inevitable but vastly overdue. The reason was very simple. If the inhabitants of a fairly advanced country with a democratic tradition and established culture find themselves shackled for years on end by the iron rules and restrictions of a stalinist bureaucracy alien to them and inferior to what they had attained in their own previous development, and when they see all their country's best prospects and resources condemned to frustration and wastage on a scale likely to make their existence as a nation and a state meaningless—then their desperation is bound to reach such a pitch that they can do nothing but revolt. And having said that, it is immediately necessary to add something else of equal importance: that if an experience of the kind just mentioned befalls Czechoslovakia, a country which, alone in Eastern Europe, had the resources to keep in being a classical bourgeois-democratic regime from the end of the First World War right up to the German occupation; a country which, again alone in Eastern Europe, harboured a Communist Party with mass membership and allowed it legal status all those years;

a country with such a well-developed sense of social justice that many of its liberal thinkers and statesmen were 'bolsheviks' in their right-wing opponents' eyes (as Beneš and Masaryk were to Hitler); a country whose entire development until that time was in the direction of socialism, so that the post-war victory of socialism was the outcome neither of some palace *putsch*, nor of a Great Power partition into spheres of influence, but of a democratic majority decision by the public—then the character and content of its revolt must needs be fixed to a great extent by all these factors.

The revolt was not, and could not be, a denial of socialism; for that, my nation would have had to deny its whole history and culture, its very essence. What it was, was a reaction to those traits of post-war socialist practice that our people were rejecting as deforming and falsifying the first socialist ideals, as something alien to the true programme.

Whatever the observer's own political position, from that of a bourgeois apologist who sees the whole socialist movement vitiated by naïveté to that of a left-wing vigilante at the opposite extreme for whom the Prague experiment was a blasphemy and a threat to the existing socialist powers, he can hardly feel any doubt about *one* aspect of the Czechoslovak 'spring'. It meant, unmistakably, a renaissance of socialism. That was its promise and its limitation. From our Czechoslovak soil nothing could have sprung but some such attempt to enrich the social ideas of the Left by granting full scope and reality to the possibilities of democracy, through which individual and sovereign nations can enter the collective stream of progress—especially those small nations who, nestling close beside the great ones and noticing their introvert and all-embracing instinct to mould others in their own shape, feel an uneasiness, no matter what universal doctrine those great ones quote.

It is a feature of public life in Czechoslovakia that the nation's thoughts, feelings and endeavours are put better by writers than by politicians. It was accordingly a writer, Milan Kundera, who depicted the 1968 spring as

an attempt finally (and for the first time in the world) to create a socialism without an omnipotent secret police; with freedom of the spoken and written word; with a public opinion of which notice is taken and on which policy is based; with a modern culture, freely developing; and with citizens who have lost their fear.

Was that too little to strive for or too much, perhaps?

Whatever the answer, we felt wonderful during those few months that our spring was crammed into; our lives were full and intense and we worked in an ecstasy of wellbeing, as if we would condense a lifetime into one short season. We published our own newspaper again. Sentenced to death in September, *Literární noviny* came back to life the following March as *Literární listy*, with the same board and the same editors, with our colleagues Klíma, Vaculík and Liehm back in charge of their old departments and myself acting as editor-in-chief again. A large section of the public realised from the special fate accorded to the old paper that it had been some kind of pioneer for 'socialism with a human face', and watched us hopefully. Our circulation rose from 120,000 to more than 300,000 copies each week. For a pretty serious literary journal among a nation of some ten million, babes and ancients excluded, the figure is an eloquent one.

For the first time in our lives we were producing a paper with no censorship and no outside dictation of ideas: nothing but our own conscience and sense of responsibility. Alas, it was to last only the few short months from March to August 1968. In retrospect we can see how impetuous our writing was, as if we had been trying to get through everything in the shortest possible space of time. Hence many a naive and imprudent word. The politician will no doubt deplore them as harmful, but the discerning reader, from a little distance, will be surely able to make out their other qualities.

The aims of the new paper, in short, were these:

We wanted to analyse the methods and meaning of the stalinist management of society, including the unprecedentedly scandalous trials of the 'fifties. These were an extreme yet typical feature of stalinism, which continued in milder but basically similar forms to affect daily life right up to January, 1968. We continued to regard the elimination of such practices, and the exposure of their roots in the police-state system, as a precondition for the establishment of any new and more just system.

We hoped to contribute positive ideas towards a programme based on an open, socialist society with legal guarantees for civic freedom, a properly functioning public opinion, politics conducted openly and not behind closed doors, a free press and a pluralistic political structure. This was to put an end to dictatorships, petty and gross, at all levels of society; to protect the public against intrigue and chicanery; and in general to bring back into political activity its prime object—the quest for justice and for the true aims of human existence.

We intended to ask questions about the proper place of literature, and of culture generally, in a new society of this kind. By publishing the best works of literature and the most serious criticism we wanted to enable literature gradually to relinquish its present role in our country—that of doing duty for political journalism under conditions of persecution—and to aspire to contribute to human thought at the highest European and world level, as our writers had done in two earlier ages.

Was all this, or any of it, a threat to socialism? Socialism had been presented to the world originally as a means of increasing human freedom by ending class discrimination. If it was obliged during the revolution and in the days immediately following it to restrict freedom, then the more time elapsed under those conditions the greater the obligation to expand it again subsequently: anything else meant a denial of socialism and its perversion into mere ideological camouflage for power wielded, in fact, on quite different principles. Relative material prosperity can be attained without socialism, as the advanced industrial countries prove; socialism can only succeed there if it can give promise of humanising otherwise utilitarian relations, of imbuing both inividual and social life with a greater sense of freedom and justice.

To this extent, then, the Czechoslovak experiment of 1968 has permanent value, whatever its further fate. It happened, and cannot be erased from the record. It will be analysed and so breed further impulses to be developed and enlarged upon in their turn, superseded and rejected. The challenge remains, however varied the response will be in different times and places. And the actual course of events in Czechoslovakia in the spring of 1968, and the reactions of other socialist countries—these too are facts to be seriously weighed and included in anyone's calculations.

For if we look today at the autumn invasion by the armies of the five Warsaw Pact countries which interrupted the progress launched in spring, we cannot say that Czechoslovakia is an occupied country with no sovereignty left, however limited her sovereignty has been since the collision. Military intervention, it seems, was the paramount form of pressure, resorted to when all other forms had been tried in vain. The pressure bears hardest on the leading politicians, though not only on them, for it reaches down into every part of society which is in any sort of contact with those leaders. It is fairly clear what the aim of such pressure is: to ensure that the leaders, whatever their own convictions, do not allow socialism in Czechoslovakia to go beyond the confines of the pattern that emerged from the October Revolution and which was prescribed, with minor modifications, for all European socialist countries after the last war. Hence the new thesis of only one permissible type of socialism: anything above or beside it must be against it—must be the work of the devil. The existence of China, Yugoslavia and Cuba, and of great communist parties like those of France and Italy, are incompatible with the thesis, but its belated proclamation only underlines the chronic state of nervous animosity that prevails between the protagonists. The Warsaw Pact invasion was the opening blow, then, in a struggle designed to reimpose on Czechoslovakia the centralist, state-power-oriented version of socialism with all that involves, such as the things our book has described. The Czechoslovak spring was an attempt to get beyond that version and to improve upon it in one country, without any thought of leaving the socialist world system, still less of breaking the obligations imposed by adherence to the Warsaw Pact. But the invasion showed with superb clarity that the Pact powers made no such distinction. The dominant socialism of the Soviet type dogmatically regards every departure from its own path as a threat to its overall interests; it sees itself entirely conditioned by a power structure appropriate to the division of the world into two camps and to the highly polarised equilibrium between the two Super-powers.

Let me return now to the 'famous sentence' at the end of the book. The foresight it implied is in no way a compliment to the author's wisdom. It simply reflected the experience of a man who has seen in clinical close-up the political system in his country being moulded over two decades according to the rules of an obligatory type of socialism, applied with scant regard to national, historic, administrative or mental differences, and with no acknowledgement of the right to different solutions for similar problems in different longitudes. At the risk of seeming immodest, then, I will venture the view that this book has lost nothing of its topicality through what has transpired since the last words in it were written. I have tried to use the conflict between the writers and the Novotný power centre as an example on which to base a tentative account of the way a reformed stalinist system operates in a crisis: my findings, if they were correct, do not cease to be relevant. Native readers are saying that they depict a standard situation found repeatedly in this part of the world. And if one were to substitute for every reference to *Literární noviny*, they tell me, a reference to the Czechoslovak spring, and for every allusion to Novotný's power centre a phrase about 'dogmatic supporters of a well-known version of socialism', then the whole opera could be repeated with this new libretto. I am not sure things are so simple. But certainly the events that followed my last chapter, the spring and then the autumn, showed stalinism in no very different light from before; they only illumined its nature more vividly than ever.

Appendix

Speeches made at the Fourth Congress of the Czechoslovak Writers' Union June 27–9, 1967

1. Milan Kundera

Dear friends! When the Union's central committee was preparing this Congress it decided to abandon the usual introductory speeches, which were always exceedingly long, authoritative and boring, and give each of you instead a written statement of its views on various topical issues of cultural policy. A lot of you contributed to this through your own suggestions, e.g. Laco Novomeský, Jaroslav Seifert, Juraj Špitzer, Kosík, Brabec, Chvatík, Števček and many others. It was discussed at two sessions of our own central committee and its penultimate version came under very heavy fire at a full meeting of the Ideological Department of the Party's Central Committee. Please don't expect anything theoretically sophisticated. The idea is much more modest, yet also much more ambitious, namely to try and get agreement on a number of elementary viewpoints the general acceptance of which, we feel, would help the further growth of our literature. Don't regard it, again, as a final text, but as a draft for our concluding resolution and as a working document, then, designed to incorporate the whole spirit of the discussion we are about to have.

One thing is missing in this draft: an evaluation of the literature produced over the past period. The omission is deliberate. We all remember so well those congresses and, in particular, those conferences where one book after another was lined up as if for Judgement Day: some were then sent on to Paradise and blissfully lost sight of, while others were consigned to Hell and are still being read. Obviously the criteria we used in those days were wrong ones, and perhaps our assessments today would be a fraction more accurate. But that isn't the point. The very principle of authoritative, institutional evaluation is, I feel, basically unsound. If any institution is capable of making a sensible decision this will be thanks to its awareness of its own limitations and its refusal to substitute its own judgement for the free process of perceiving values. Our own Union for one has no desire to displace that long-term process of literary appreciation, involving the whole gamut of critics and theorists. It feels not the slightest obligation to back *Impuls* against *Orientace* or *Orientace* against *Impuls*, to support Jarmila Glazarová versus Bohumil Hrabal or vice versa. Our central committee realises that its job is to enable everyone to express his opinion and carry on a free argument. And it knows from bitter experience that it is much harder to provide guarantees of this kind than to pass snap judgements about a process which, in terms of human life, is never-ending.

Still, there is one general judgement about the writings of the last four years which will probably stand up fairly well. It has been a period of expansion. I hope I need not document this point with a list of titles. We all know the output and each of us has his own preferences. The main thing is that a variety of works appeared—good works in great number—and that some fields like the cinema (which largely belongs to literature and concerns us therefore) have flourished as never before in the country's history.

For Czech and Slovak literature, and probably for Czech art altogether, these have been the best years since 1948 : perhaps since 1938. The best for thirty years, then. This ratio—four to thirty—represents the grim side of an otherwise gratifying verdict and is something to remember, I suggest, as a footnote to all our thoughts and worries.

Seeing that I am up here on the platform, perhaps you would allow me at this point to give you my own thoughts, and you can count this as my contribution to the debate. I shall only be talking about Czech problems, but I am sure that what I say applies to Slovak problems too.

Dear friends! No nation has been on earth since the beginning of time and the very concept of nationhood is pretty recent. Despite that, most nations look upon their own existence as a self-evident destiny conferred by God, or by Nature, since time immemorial. Nations tend to think of their cultures and political systems, even their frontiers, as the work of Man, but they see their national existence as a transcendent fact, beyond all question. The somewhat cheerless and intermittent history of the Czech nation, which has passed through the very antechamber of death, gives us the strength to resist any such illusion. For there has never been anything self-evident about the existence of the Czech nation and one of its most distinctive traits, in fact, has been the *unobviousness* of that existence.

This emerged most clearly in the early nineteenth century when a handful of intellectuals tried to resurrect our half-forgotten language and then, a generation later, our half-moribund people too. The resurrection was a deliberate act and, like every act, involved a choice between the arguments *for* and *against*. The thinkers of the Czech Revival, though they decided in favour, knew the arguments on the other side as well. They realised as Matouš Klácel for one pointed out, that germanisation would provide an easier life for the Bohemian populace and better career prospects for its children. They knew that belonging to the majority people gave more opportunity for more influential brainwork, whereas using the Czech language, as Klácel admitted, meant that 'fewer people will be acquainted with the scholar's efforts'. They were well aware of the tribulations of small nations who, to quote Kollár, 'think by halves and feel by halves', and whose culture is 'usually petty and stunted, not fully alive but only clinging on to life without growth or blossom, merely vegetating and sending up suckers but no sturdy trunks'.

This consciousness of the balance of argument meant that the question 'To be or not to be? And if so, why?' was built into the very foundations of modern Czech history. When the men of the Revival opted for 'To be', this was a great challenge to the future. It now fell to the nation to justify their choice in the course of its own history.

It marched well with the logic of this basic *unobviousness* in Czech life that Hubert Gordon Schauer, in 1886, should fling in the face of the Czech community (a small one, but already snuggling cosily back into its own pettiness) those shocking questions of his.

Should we not have contributed more to mankind, he asked, if we had harnessed our spiritual energies to the culture of a great nation, a culture already flourishing on a far higher plane than our own embryonic affair? Had the re-establishment of the nation really been worth the bother? Was the cultural worth of the Czechs great enough to justify their existence as a nation? And secondly, was it great enough to save them from denationalisation at some later date?

Czech provincialism, quite content to go on vegetating, naturally regarded this conversion of certainties into question-marks as an attack on the nation, and accordingly cast him out. Yet only five years later the young critic Šalda was calling Schauer the greatest figure of his generation and describing the article in question as a patriotic deed in the truest sense of the word. Nor was he mistaken. For Schauer, after all, had only put a sharp point to what the great revivalists knew the whole time. 'Unless', wrote Palacký, 'we exalt our own nation's spirit to higher and nobler activities than those of our neighbours, we shall not preserve even our natural prerogatives.' And Neruda insisted that 'it is our duty now to set our nation on a level of awareness and education equal to the rest of the world, and not merely so as to win recognition for it but to assure its very survival'.

The men of the Revival saw the nation's existence as dependent on those cultural values which the nation might create. They measured these values, moreover, not in terms of their direct utility to the nation alone but by the criteria—as we used to say—of universal humanity. They wanted to belong to the world and to Europe. And this reminds me of something quite peculiar to Czech literature, which has given rise to a type of man very rare in other literatures, namely the translator as a significant, even a dominant, literary personality. For when you come to think of it the biggest literary figures in the century before the Battle of the White Mountain were all translators: Řehoř Hrubý of Jelení, the first translator of Erasmus anywhere, Daniel Adam of Veleslavín, or Jan Blahoslav. Jungmann's celebrated translation of Milton is a foundation-stone of Revivalist Czech. Our output of translations from foreign languages is still among the finest in the world and translators in our country have the status of literary personalities. It is clear why such an important role was assigned to translation: it was the practice of translation which enabled Czech to mould and perfect itself as a language on a par with other European languages and in possession of a European vocabulary. Moreover, it was in the form of translations that Czechs had been making their own, Czech-language, contribution to European literature and that literature had been acquiring its own, Czech-reading, European readers.

For those European nations who partook in the mainstream of history the European context comes quite naturally. But Czech history displays an alternation of periods of wakefulness with periods of sleep, so that we missed several important phases in the development of the European spirit and every time were obliged to acquire it again at second hand and fill it out for ourselves. For the Czechs nothing was ever a self-evident possession: not even their language nor their European status. Their participation in Europe was an eternal dilemma: whether to allow Czech to degenerate into a mere European dialect and Czech culture into mere European folklore, or to be one of the nations of Europe with all that that implies.

The second course alone can guarantee true survival. But this was an extraordinarily difficult course for a nation which throughout the nineteenth century had perforce devoted most of its energies to laying foundation-stones—everything from secondary schools to the Encyclopedia. Yet at the beginning of the twentieth century, and especially in the inter-war period, a cultural blossoming took place quite unprecedented in Czech history. In the brief space of twenty years a whole constellation of geniuses fell to creating works that raised Czech culture, in all its individuality, up to European standards again for the first time since the age of Comenius.

This great period, so short and intense that it still awakens nostalgia in our hearts, was for all that a period of adolescence, of course, rather than maturity. Czech writing was still predominantly lyrical; it was still limbering up and all it needed was time, peaceful and free from disturbance. That the growth of such a tender culture should have been interrupted for nearly a quarter of a century altogether, first by the German occupation, and then, close on its heels, by stalinism, isolating it from the outside world, cutting short many of its varied domestic traditions and degrading it to the level of sheer propaganda—this was a tragedy that bade fair to relegate the Czech nation once more, and this time permanently, to the cultural periphery of Europe. If in the past few years Czech culture has taken a new leap forward and today constitutes the most successful aspect of the nation's activity; if many outstanding works have appeared and some branches of art, such as the cinema, are achieving higher standards than ever before; then it is this which ranks as the paramount national event of the past period.

Yet is the community in any way appreciative of the fact? Does it realise that the opportunity has come to continue the great adolescence of our inter-war literature, and that this opportunity can never come again? Does it realise that the fate of our culture is its own fate? Is the belief of the Revivalists any less true today, that the nation's existence cannot be guaranteed without solid cultural values?

The national role of culture has certainly changed since the Revival and we are hardly threatened with national oppression today. Yet I believe that culture is no whit less essential for us as the nation's justification and surety. In the second half of the twentieth century we have seen the great prospects of integration opening up. Human progress has been for the first time fused into a single world-wide development. Small units are combining into larger ones. International cultural efforts are being concentrated and coordinated. Travelling has become a mass activity. With all this, the role of a few world languages, the most important ones, becomes enhanced, and the more international every part of our lives becomes, the more restricted is the field for the languages of small nations. I was talking recently to a Flemish-speaking Belgian, a theatrical worker who complained about the threat to his native tongue. The Flemish intelligentsia, he said, was becoming bilingual and giving preference to English as the road to more direct contact with foreign academic life. In such a situation a small nation can only protect its language and its individuality by the cultural standing of that language, by the uniqueness of the values it has created and which the world associates it with. Plzen beer, of course, is also a 'value'. The trouble is that the outside world drinks it under the German name of Pilsner Urquell. Pilsner is not enough to justify the Czech's claim to have a language of their own. And the world of the future, as unification proceeds, will quite ruthlessly and quite rightly ask us to present our accounts and justify the existence we chose for ourselves a hundred and fifty years ago, and will ask us why we made that choice.

It is of paramount importance that our whole national community should be fully aware how vitally essential to us our culture and literature are. For Czech literature—and this is another of its special features—has very little of the aristocratic about it: it is a plebeian literature closely linked to the wide national public. That is its strength and its weakness. Its strength, in that it affords it background of firm support where its language finds a clear echo; its weakness, because it is not yet emancipated from the public's level of education and liberality of mind and is highly susceptible to any displays of popular philistinism. I sometimes dread that our present-day culture may be losing that European standard which the Czech humanists and Revivalists had in mind. The world of Graeco-Roman antiquity and the world of Christianity, those two mainsprings of the European spirit which give it its strength and tension, have almost disappeared from the consciousness of the educated young Czech—an irremediable loss. For there is an iron continuity in European thought that outlasts each intellectual revolution and has created its own vocabulary, its own fund of metaphor, its own myths and themes, without knowledge of which cultured Europeans cannot communicate. I read a horrifying report recently describing the knowledge of world literature attained by our future teachers of Czech. I should hate to be told what their familiarity with world history is like. Provincialism is not just a literary trend; it is first and foremost a problem that effects the whole life of the country, starting with its schools and its newspapers.

I recently saw the film *Sedmikrásky* (*The Daisies*) which tells of two gloriously repulsive girls, smugly satisfied with their own delightful mediocrity and gaily wrecking everything that transcended their own horizon. It struck me that what I was watching was a very topical parable with far-reaching implications, a parable about vandalism. Who are the vandals today? Not your illiterate peasant setting fire to the hated landlord's mansion in a fit of rage. The vandals I see around me these days are well off, educated people, satisfied with themselves and bearing no particular grudge. The vandal is a man proud of his mediocrity, very much at ease with himself and ready to insist on his democratic rights. In his pride and his mediocrity he imagines that one of his inalienable privileges is to transform the world after his own image, and since the most important things in this world are the innumerable things that transcend his vision, he adjusts the world to his own image by destroying it. A youngster knocks the head off a statue in the park because the statue insults him with its more-than-human size, and it gives him pleasure to do so because every act of self-assertion gives a man satisfaction. People who live purely in their own immediate present tense, without culture or awareness of historical continuity, are quite capable of turning their country into a wasteland with no history, no memory, no echo or beauty. Vandalism today assumes more forms than those the police can prosecute. If the public's legal representatives, or the competent officials, decide that a statue, a castle, a church or a hundred-year-old lime-tree is superfluous and order its removal, this is just another form of the same vandalism. There is basically no difference between legal and illegal destruction, between destruction and prohibition. A Czech deputy recently asked in Parliament on behalf of twenty-one other deputies for the prohibition of two serious and intelligent Czech films. One of them ironically, was this parable of the vandals, *Sedmikrásky*. He inveighed brutally against both films, while positively boasting that he understood neither of them. The contradiction in such an attitude is only on the surface. The two works had chiefly offended by transcending the human horizons of their judges, so that they were felt as an insult. (Applause.)

In a letter to Helvetius, Voltaire has the marvellous sentence: 'I do not agree with what you are saying, but I will fight to the death for your right to say it.' This is one way of putting the basic moral principle of modern civilisation. To go back in history beyond this principle is to take a step from the modern period into the Middle Ages. All suppression of opinions, including the forcible suppression of wrong opinions, is hostile to truth in its consequences. For the truth can only be reached by a dialogue of free opinions enjoying equal rights. Any interference with freedom of thought and word, however discreet the mechanics and terminology of such censorship, is a scandal in this century, a chain entangling the limbs of our national literature as it tries to bound forward.

One thing is surely indisputable. If our art has blossomed, it is because intellectual freedom has increased. The fate of Czech literature is vitally dependent, just now, on the degree of intellectual freedom that exists. As soon as one mentions 'freedom', of course, some people seem to have a fit of hay-fever and object that freedom must have its limits in a socialist literature. Why naturally, every freedom has its limits imposed, say, by the state of contemporary knowledge, or education, or prejudice and so forth. But no new progressive movement has ever described itself by its own limitations! The Renaissance did not define itself in terms of the cramping naïveté of its rationalism, which only became apparent after a lapse of time, but in terms of its rationalistic transcendence of previous limitations. Romanticism saw itself as a crossing of the frontiers set by the canons of classicism, as the new territory won beyond those frontiers. And the expression 'socialist literature' will have no positive meaning until it, too, implies a liberating transcendence of limits.

In our society it is counted a greater virtue to guard the frontiers than to cross them. The most transitory political and social considerations are used to justify all kinds of constraint on our intellectual liberty. But great policies are policies that set the interest of the age above the interest of the moment. The quality of Czech culture is, for the Czech nation, the interest of a whole epoch.

This is all the truer at a time when the nation is faced with quite exceptional opportunities. In the nineteenth century we lived on the margin of world history. In this century we live in its very mid-point. This, we are well aware, is no bed of roses. But the miraculous soil of art turns suffering into gold. It even turns the bitter experience of stalinism into a paradoxical, indispensable asset. I hate to hear stalinism equated with fascism. Fascism, based on undisguised anti-humanism, brought about a fairly simple moral situation; it left the humane principles and virtues untouched, for it presented itself as their antithesis. But stalinism was heir to a great humane movement which, even amidst the stalinist malaise, preserved some of its attitudes, its thoughts, its slogans, language and dreams. To see such a movement degenerate in front of one's eyes into something quite contrary and strip itself of every human virtue, to see it turn love for humanity into cruelty toward people, turn love for truth into denunciation and the like—this was to witness unbelievable aspects of basic human values and qualities. What is history? What is Man in history? What, indeed, is Man at all? No one could give the same answer to any of these questions *after* experiencing such changes as before. No one left this episode of history the same man as he entered it. And stalinism, of course, is not the only issue. The whole course of our nation's history, torn between democracy, fascist enslavement, stalinism and socialism, and further complicated by its unique nationality problem, features every important issue that has made our twentieth century what it is. This enables us, perhaps, to put more searching questions and create more significant myths than people who have not undergone such an anabasis. Our nation then has experienced, I daresay, more than many others have in this century and, if its genius has been alert, it will now know more than the others. This greater know-ledge might prove to be that liberating transcendence of old limits, that crossing of the boundaries of traditional wisdom about Man and his destiny which could confer upon Czech culture a meaning, maturity and greatness. So far these are only prospects, possibilities—but perfectly realistic ones, as many a work created during the past few years has shown.

Once more, however, we must put the question: Is our public aware of these possibilities? Does it know that they are its own possibilities? Does it know that history never offers such chances twice? Does it know that to miss the chance means to let slip the whole of this century for our Czech nation?

'It is a matter of general knowledge', wrote Palacký, 'that it was the Czech writers who, instead of letting the nation perish, brought it to life again and gave it noble aims to accomplish.' It is the Czech writers who were responsible for the very existence of the nation and remain so today. For it is upon the standard of Czech literature, its greatness or meanness, its courage or cowardice, its provincialism or its universality, that the answer to the nation's existential question largely depends, namely: Is its survival worth while? Is the survival of its language worth while?

These, the most fundamental questions at the very roots of our latter-day nationhood, are still awaiting a definitive answer. Everyone who, by his bigotry, his vandalism, his want of culture or liberality, thwarts the new blossoming of our culture, threatens the very life of the nation as well.

2. Laco Novomeský (read in his absence by Vojtech Mihálik)
Dear conference members! You must have noticed—but if it escaped you, I should like to draw your attention to it—that the report on the activity of our Czechoslovak and Slovak Writers' Unions dwells in several passages on the tricky problem of the Union's own periodicals, particularly the Slovak *Kultúrny život* and the Czech *Literární noviny*. 'The Union's committees have devoted a great deal of time to the question of its periodicals. Almost every meeting had some problem in this connection on its agenda . . .' says the report, speaking for Prague and for Bratislava alike.

I took part myself in the meetings of the Slovak Union's committee in connection with *Kultúrny život* in particular, and since the discussion mainly concerned the editors' complaints about interference by the Press Control I should like to speak principally about this.

The Third Congress of the Czechoslovak Writers' Union instructed the Union's committee (and this applies to the Slovak Union's committee too) 'to devote most of its discussions to ideological and artistic questions affecting Czechoslovak literature . . .' Since we had to talk about *Kultúrny život*, however, our deliberations never got beyond the stage of indignation over the Press Control's latest inroads on our periodical.

The editor-in-chief would arrive at the committee meeting with a whole packet of articles and proofsheets that had been held up by Press Control in the previous weeks, whereupon we committee members were supposed to devote ourselves to 'ideological and artistic questions', as well as political ones and so on, directly or indirectly related to literature up as far as the boundary line prescribed by the Press Control officials.

Daily experience, especially among us Slovaks, taught us to see the light side of this absurd situation and tolerate it somewhat. If we did not understand why Press Control had objected to this or that article we would entrust the editor-in-chief or some other Union official to ask the appropriate Department of the Communist Party's Central Committee either to explain the reasons or to release the article. It was the experience of *Kultúrny život*—not in every case, but almost always—that whenever Press Control had to think hard why it wanted to stop an article, and then the Writers' Union committee had to think why the authorities had had to stop it, and finally a lot of thinking and explaining had taken place in the relevant Party Department, then the article saw the light of day after all. It was enough to make a few minor corrections, not affecting the substance of the article, and it would appear in the very same number of *Kultúrny život*.

We got so accustomed to this procedure that every time the paper's difficulties with Press Control came up for discussion we would casually assume that the Union's officials would manage by argument or prayer to get the article in question passed, and we were not unduly worried whether it would appear in the issue it was written for or only a week or three weeks later. The Czech weekly *Literární noviny*, as we can tell from the report presented to this Congress, was not able to benefit from tactics of this kind. 'Remonstrations against Press Control measures', we read, 'were for the most part unsuccessful'.

I have not seen these 'wicked' articles. However, I know *Literární noviny* and have read articles in it which had provoked indignation, if not a strict anathema, on the part of Press Control. They were all articles which made one think, or invited the reader to ponder them—surely welcome qualities in socialist and democratic publications.

Though I certainly wouldn't claim the right, on the basis of these impressions, to pronounce absolution over these papers, it does seem to me that they are written not by insidious saboteurs but by authors whose sense of responsibility can be trusted.

One cannot help wondering, then, whether the writer's sense of responsibility would not be a more reliable instrument for controlling the press than this special institution which either, in the more favourable case as we saw, delays a production process that is slow enough already, or else tries to stop something that is essentially unstoppable. Let me put it more precisely. My view is that in place of the institution, under whatever name, of press control, a more reliable and dignified tool would be the socialist, democratic sense of responsibility of the author or authors of the paper, magazine, book or other publication—especially here in Czechoslovakia. I shall mention a few factors which weigh particularly in favour of a 'radical' reform of journalistic control on these lines.

First, the very existence of Press Control seriously hampers the growth of all journalism and art, however broadminded it is and even if it refrains from holding up manuscripts or articles and even of books, as we have learnt from time to time. For in itself it creates 'self-censorship', forcing authors not to write, and indeed not to think, about and analyse problems, if the products 'would be censored anyway' or almost certainly so.

In any adult society, wherever there is press control there is an 'illicit' literature of things which have been or might be prohibited. I can think of nothing worse or more discreditable to us than the existence, or non-existence as it were, of unwritten books and articles about problems which attract potential authors, who however postpone or abandon the hopeless labour of working out 'unsuitable' ideas because they know they could never be published. Lenin himself favoured more tolerant and concessive treatment of writers, and that in a period of time incomparably more dangerous and complex than our own. It was not that he wanted to show special favour to literature and to writers; it was clearly that he realised how much the progress of literature, and the understanding and analysis of the problems literature has to deal with, requires above all an atmosphere of freedom in which nothing and nobody interferes.

Secondly, by whatever names it is known and whoever, anywhere, exercises it, control over the press gravely compromises our socialist system by its very existence, and in the particular Czechoslovak case by its method of application as well. In the past few years our literature has undergone remarkable progress. Today's reader is not satisfied with what were normal standards five years ago and it is certainly to the credit of those responsible for our cultural policies that they do not feebly insist on what the reader has rejected, but are flexible enough to meet his healthy demands. Let me quote the case of Škvorecký's novel *Zbabělci* (*The Cowards*), not long ago rejected with scorn for reasons that were partly, perhaps mainly, political, and now not merely permitted on the same grounds but praised to the skies and deservedly appreciated. I do not deny the rights of those critics who wrongly condemned the novel. But why did the state and the Party with its various institutions have to get involved in the matter, when the humiliation which the over-hasty critics, in this case, deservedly suffered was quite sufficient by itself? Especially in artistic matters, after all, there are no eternal, rigid criteria for a controlling authority with executive powers confidently to apply in assessing books and magazine articles or in other fields—films, plays, music and dancing. Our cultural policy itself keeps reminding us that there are no such criteria, so why the control?

I think the time has come to liberate literature and other art forms like the cinema, to liberate journalism and also to liberate the state and Party from the burden that sits so uneasily upon them in the form of 'control', whatever it is called. For whether it is strict or lenient it either compromises our socialist system or convicts itself of futility. I think the time has come to put our trust in the civic and socialist spirit of those who write books and magazine articles, criticise films or make them, or produce other kinds of art. I think this time has come.

What is typical in Czech and Slovak literature is a sense of social involvement in the problems of our nations and of our own day. But I do not think it is absolutely necessary that a writer should divide and indeed dissipate his energy between his own craft and drawing up manifestos on topical political or philosophical subjects. Let us leave each author to decide how he wants to show his excitement about issues which excite, or ought to excite, each of us; let him decide whether to show it in the poem itself or 'merely' in its nuances, its tone or mood or whatever. Our paramount demand is this: Don't pretend you can ignore and overlook the things which inspire every other kind of civic activity. Ignoring and overlooking is a form of involvement too—but on the other side, the adversary's. The writer can find his own way of expressing his outlook and we should be doing him violence if we tried to decide it for him.

The cultural front, and especially the literary front, has always played a big part in Czech-Slovak relations, and so it does today. How should Slovak and Czech writers try to contribute towards setting out and solving problems in this field?

Czech writers can help by spontaneously realising and consistently, day by day, unrhetorically (not just by once-for-all statements) persuading the Czech public to realise its responsibility in making sure that the Slovaks, living in this alliance with them, do not feel themselves to be a tolerated race of vice-chairmen and deputy-ministers, a second-class minority generously accorded a one-third quota in everything, but a partner with equal rights and of equal value: a nation which in many ways is only now completing its own growth and putting the final touches to its individuality. The Czech public must not bridle at this process but accept it with understanding, in the interest of its own freedom, and selflessly assist it.

And the Slovaks for their part can help by criticising and publicly condemning the spread of self-complacency on their own territory and among their own kin, who are getting intolerably big for their boots; for this is one way of making the national character stronger and healthier, and we shall never get our rightful place in the sun by shouting and lamenting, still less by beating our chests and reciting about our glorious past and saying what incomparably fine fellows we are.

Our Fourth Congress ought to have a look at this question. It really ought to. Or if not this Congress, then one of the next ones. (Applause.)

3. Ludvík Vaculík

I am using this opportunity, comrades, to tell you something you know already, since I have a few practical suggestions to make about it. In the draft Standpoint it is said that the purpose of a socialist system is to effect the reintegration of man, as guaranteed by the civil code. 'Citizen' was once a glorious and revolutionary word. It meant a man whom no one could arbitrarily order about, a man who could only be governed cunningly, so that he almost believed he was governing himself. To succeed in making this impression on the subjects of government was the purpose, in past ages, of that highly skilled craft known as politics. In reality, the citizen who ruled over himself was a myth, and will always be one.

The Marxist critique of power dragged out into the light of day relationships, hitherto unexamined, between the ruling power and the ownership of means of production. This discovery, together with an understanding of human history as the history of class warfare, laid the way for a social revolution which was expected to provide a new solution of the eternal problem of power. In our country the social revolution succeeded: and the problem of power continues. Though we have 'taken the bull by the horns' and still hold him fast, someone keeps kicking us in the backside and won't stop.

It seems that power has its own inviolable laws of development and behaviour, regardless of who exercises it. Power is a peculiar human phenomenon, due to the fact that even in the jungle someone in the tribe has to give the orders, and even in the most high-minded community someone has to sum up the discussion and draft the priorities. Power is a characteristically human situation. It hits the rulers and the ruled, and is good for the health of neither. Thousands of years of experience persuaded men to try to lay down rules of procedure. Hence the system of formal democracy with its feedbacks and control switches and limiting values. But the neatly designed mechanism of government is confronted with the interests of men equipped with brute strength based on ownership of capital, or possession of weapons, or family influence, or industrial monopoly, and so on. So the rules of procedure do not prevent evil, and it only takes a slight distortion to turn this observation into the crude assertion that the rules of formal democracy create evil. But the rules in themselves are neither capitalist nor socialist; they do not decide what should be done, but how to reach a decision on what to do. They are a human invention which makes the job of ruling considerably harder. They favour the ruled, but when a government falls they also save its ministers from being shot. The maintenance of such a formal system of democracy does not bring strong government, but it brings the conviction that the next government may be better. So the government can fall, but the citizen is renewed. In places, by contrast, where governments are long-lasting, it is the citizen who falls. How far does he fall? I will not oblige the enemy by saying that he falls victim to the executioner. That only happens to a few dozen or a few hundred in the country.

But even our friends know that this is enough. For then the whole nation may fall into a panic, into political apathy or civic resignation, succumb to trivial daily cares and petty cravings and dependence upon masters at lower and lower levels, and in short turn into serfs of a new kind, so strange that you cannot even explain it to a foreign visitor. In our country I do not think there are any citizens these days. I have my reasons for saying this, based on years of work in the press and radio. I need not go very far to lay hands on one brand new reason. This Congress did not take place when the members of our organisation wanted it to, but when the master, after weighing up his own worries, kindly gave his consent. In return he expects—as thousands of years of history have led him to expect—that we pay homage to his dynasty. I propose that we don't. I propose we take a good look at the text of the Standpoint and cross out everything that smells of serfdom. Among nations that have nurtured their civilisation on criticism of the ruling power it ill befits the writers, of all people, to forget what their sensible popular education has taught them.

I suggest that every subsequent speaker at this Congress should say how he would like things to be in the field he is concerned about. Let us play at being citizens, seeing we have been given permission and a playground; for the rest of our time, let us make speeches as if we were grown up and legally independent.

I speak here as the citizen of a state which I will never abandon, but in which I cannot contentedly live. I am thinking of civic matters, but I shall find myself in a delicate situation. As a member of the Communist Party I am not supposed to talk here about Party business, nor do I propose to. What has happened in this country, though, is that there is hardly anything which at a certain stage of the argument does not become Party business. What am I to do if the two institutions—my own government and my own Party—have done their best to make their respective agenda identical? Personally I think it is a bad move for both of them. It also creates a difficult situation for those of us citizens who are gathered here today. Party members are under obligation to keep silent about the crucial points of most of our serious problems in the presence of non-members, and these last are barred from attending the only forum where they can be meaningfully discussed. As a result, both members and non-members suffer under a permanent limitation of one basic civic freedom—the freedom to talk as equals with other citizens. Perhaps this is even a violation of the Twentieth Article of the Constitution. However, I shall observe discipline and retreat to civic territory; I shall just be talking about the government and only when this term is unsuitable shall I use the phrase 'ruling circles'. Though seemingly vague, this latter is an old and well-tried term and more precise than any other. It has been used from time immemorial to describe the people who really ruled, regardless of their nominal function in the façade of democracy; people whose strength flowed from elsewhere—from riches, from favour and influence, from a monopoly of production or service, from the possession of arms and so on. And the term also covers government exercised from private theatre boxes, sudden messages sent by special courier at night, the dropping of a few weighty remarks in the foyer or corridor so that agreements are reached before the partners even come to the table and laws are passed before the deputies have entered the chamber.

The whole history of our two nations prepared us for socialism. After the last war the state was set up again as a political organism with nothing else to do than get this socialism organised. Leaving aside some important issues affecting one or another group, this was really the only matter on the agenda after 1945. One of the assumed attributes of the new system of power was the unity, or in fact the identity, of the rulers and the ruled. 'The people and the government march forward. . . .'

But to return to my feeling about the character of power everywhere. Its development and behaviour are governed by its own special laws, regardless of what person is in power or what class is in power; they are simply the laws of human behaviour in a particular situation, namely being in power.

The first law of power is its desire to continue. It reproduces itself in ever more faithful copies. Secondly, power is forever homogenising itself, getting rid of everything alien to itself, till every part is an image of the whole and all parts are interchangeable, so that each peripheral cell of power can for practical purposes deputise for the centre and you can swap those peripheral cells around without anything going wrong. The apparatus of power goes on functioning undisturbed, because it is really not intended to react to changes in the environment at all—altitude above sea-level, population patterns or anything else. Or rather, it is intended to react to everything in the same way, by adjusting these various different environments to suit itself, by making them all identical so that it can get by with a single, superbly simple model. Power makes itself independent—this is another of its laws. It does not ask for anyone's support because it leans on itself, the centre on the periphery and vice versa. They can rely on each other with perfect confidence, indeed they have to, because they constitute a circle. No one can be removed from the circle and the circle will never let anyone go. Any domestic discord or misbehaviour is firmly dealt with—domestically.

Then comes the next phase, known as dynasty-making. At a favourable moment the wielders of power summon the legislature and have their independent status incorporated in the Constitution. After that, whatever they do is constitutional. Since they won't raise this issue again for another ten or twenty or fifty years, and nobody else according to the Constitution can raise it for them, and nobody according to the same Constitution can summon any other lawgivers, you arrive by constitutional means at the establishment of a dynasty. This is a dynasty of a historically new type, for it includes one important principle of democracy: Anyone who cares to can join in. So the dynasty can never die out, neither on the sword side nor the distaff.

The most interesting law of power for us is something that has been described in books a thousand times in the course of human history, but always remains the same—its way of dealing with people. Power prefers people of the same inner constitution as itself. But since these are in short supply, it has to make use of other people too and adjust them to its needs. The most serviceable subjects are, naturally enough, people who themselves long for power, and then people who are obedient by their very nature, people with a bad conscience, and people whose appetite for comfort, advantage and profit acknowledges no moral limits. Other people who can be adjusted are those saddled with fear and large families, those who have been humiliated in the past and trustfully accept the prospect of renewed pride, and again people who were born stupid. For a certain time, in certain circumstances and for certain purposes one can make temporary use of various moral absolutists and altruistic but ill-informed enthusiasts like myself. There are several familiar, basic techniques for adjusting people. Physical and intellectual temptation, the threat of suffering, involvement in compromising situations, the use of informers, the casting of unjust suspicions so as to provoke demonstrations of loyalty, or the method of putting people at the mercy of un-scrupulous individuals and then hypocritically rescuing them. There is the spreading of general distrust. Trust is classified as first, second or third class, the great majority of people (it is assumed) feeling no confidence about anything. Information is similarly classified by quality and issued accordingly—on pink paper, green paper, yellow paper, or newspaper. (Laughter.)

What I have said about the nature of power was meant in the most general way. I am not even thinking about government in a socialist state, for I associate socialism in my mind with scientific management and a scientific theory of socialism would be unthink-able, after all, without the psychology of power. Just as it must include philosophy, economics and sociology, so it must cover the psychology of power, making use of the findings of individual and social psychology, psychoanalysis and psychopathology.

I have skirted the question of the class character of power, because in my treatment I include this in the consideration of power as a whole.

The selection of people, as I have described it, for their service-ability to the wielders of power is something which has taken place in our country as in others. Preference has been accorded to obedient people, to people who make no difficulties and ask none of the current questions. At every stage of selection it has been the most mediocre men who showed up best while more complex creatures, people with personal charm, and above all those whose work and qualities had made them, by silent unwritten consensus, a touchstone of general decency and public conscience—these gradually disappeared from the scene. Notable absentees from political life were personalities with a sense of humour or with ideas of their own. Certain words and phrases lost their meaning altogether: 'political thinker', say, or 'representative', or 'advocate' of this or that. And 'movement' came to have a hollow ring since nothing moved. The fabric that had constituted the invisible structure and personal culture of such human communities as the village, factory or workshop—this was torn to shreds. Nothing bore the stamp of individual effort any more and the very notion of a 'workshop' almost died out. Headmasters, labouring at their pedagogic craft, were thrown out of their schools; managers of brickworks were dismissed for holding critical views about the surrounding scenery; well-supported cultural circles and sports clubs, that for certain kinds of people had afforded a whole range of continuity in their parish, their region and their country—these were simply dissolved.

In his book *Divoška Jája* Benjamin Klička wrote: 'Remember, man, that competence is an impertinent insult to your superior. So try to be dumber than the ox, and you may enjoy long life and have a happy time in this world.' I could recite these words by heart, so many times have I recalled them. They were written forty years ago and their author was thinking of society as it was before the revolution. But they have only acquired their full force, I think, since the revolution and everyone has now had a chance to appreciate their truth. I don't know whether you have noticed it, but all of us, Czechs and Slovaks, wherever we work, are inclined to believe that the men who tell us what to do are less competent than ourselves. And whenever we gather together, we all have a good grouse. It's an unattractive scene, because alongside those who may have good cause to complain the grousers include the most incapable layabouts, utter slackers and simpletons, all lamenting about what they are prevented from doing. In this way a spurious and harmful solidarity arises between people who have nothing really in common. We are linked together by the most pathetic bond anyone could imagine: the bond of shared aversion, though the motives are quite disparate.

Practical souls find themselves other fields of activity, unpractical souls nurse their martyrs' haloes. In the literary market depression, spiritual breakdown and nihilism are all the rage. There is an orgy of snobbery. Even clever people can turn stupid. They sometimes feel an instinctive need to preserve themselves, an itch to lash out left and right. But then they look up and see what hangs above them, and look down and see what could still rise up and tread *them* underfoot, and they say to themselves, What good would it do anyone, for God's sake?

Now let us consider that for twenty years the people most successful in promoting themselves have been those who put up least resistance to the demoralising effects of power. And let us consider further that those with tender consciences can find no support or grounds for appeal in the law, which ought really to protect them. For if we were to take the law literally we would believe that our country had a valid code of rights and duties calculated to promote the 'free all-round development and exercise of every citizen's personality and, at the same time, the reinforcement and progress of socialist society' (Article 19 of the Constitution).

In my newspaper and radio work I have come to the conclusion that members of the public only too often refrain from appealing to their constitutional rights for the reason that pretty well any official, central or even peripheral, is in a position to make that right dependent on circumstances and conditions which are not mentioned in the Constitution and could not with any decency be set down there.

I have recently taken to browsing through the Constitution and have decided that it is a badly constructed work and that this may be why it has lost its authority with the public and with official circles alike. As regards style, it is very wordy yet manages to be vague in many important details. I shall quote an example from the area of work and thought that most concerns our Union. Article 16 runs as follows: 'All cultural policy in Czechoslovakia, the expansion of education, training and general upbringing are conducted in the spirit of the scientific world-outlook, marxleninsim, and in close association with the life and labour of the people.' Apart from the fact that the term 'upbringing' will itself, for any good teacher, presuppose 'close association with life and labour', I cannot see what organ, or what court perhaps, is to decide whether a particular view is scientific or not. For the very concept of science involves movement and changes of view in accordance with advancing knowledge, and this mobility is contrary to the universal requirement of legal language that terms should be unambiguous and unchanging. Unless, of course, by a 'scientific world view' one means a rigid set of axioms. But that would surely make our state a doctrinaire one rather than the scientifically governed one which our legislators, I take it, had in mind.

Here is another example, affecting my own subject. Article 28 says this. 'In accordance with the interests of the working people, freedom of expression is guaranteed to all citizens in every social field, especially freedom of speech and publication.' My own view is that the kinds of freedom mentioned are intrinsically in the interest of the working people, so that the wording is tautologous and indeed confusing: it leaves it open to anyone to define what the worker's interest is. I feel that any specialist who had occasion to use that expression would need to have spelled out what is and what is not in the worker's interest, while a cautious legislator would avoid a general definition and insist on one that enumerated cases. For my part I should prefer some laconic formula that excluded all argument. It takes terse, neat wording to give laws a universal, proverbial ring ensuring them an ultimate place in the wisdom of the old folks, and to create an awareness of the law so automatic that justice can be determined almost without the aid of judges. It is the verbal sloppiness of the Constitution and the cruding thinking in it which make it impossible to ensure its observance. As things are, this primary framework of our legislation has the character of a well-intentioned political programme rather than of any legal guarantee of civic rights. The Constitution should in any case, I think, function like any other norm, with the additional proviso that in this case no subordinate norm, regulation, resolution or implementing paragraph of any kind can limit or obscure its binding force.

I have explained my ideas about the nature, development and behaviour of power in general and I have tried to show that the control mechanisms supposed to constrain it are failing to work, so that the citizen is losing his self-respect and indeed, objectively speaking, his very civic status. Whenever this state of affairs lasts as long as it has already lasted in our own country, it naturally eats into the minds of many people and above all into the lifelong attitudes of the young, who are unaware from their studies or from personal experience that there is a certain continuity about man's tottering pursuit of an ideal democracy. If this were to continue much longer, and failed to provoke the natural defence reaction, then the very character of our two nations would change in the next generation. Instead of a tough and cultured community of people we should find an easily governed populace whom it would be sheer delight, even for foreigners, to rule over. It was hardly necessary for us to spend a thousand years being obstreperous, only to end up like this.

Assuming, then, that none of us was born to make life easy for his rulers, I propose that the Writers' Union take the initiative, perhaps in collaboration with the Journalists' Union and other bodies with similar concerns, ask the Czechoslovak Academy of Science for an expert assessment of the Constitution and, if it turns out to be necessary, make suggestions for amending it. The Union might, for example, recommend members to attend preparatory meetings before the next elections, raise all these issues and try to ensure that all candidates are alive to them. Alternatively, each of us might pay a call on his deputy at any time and ask him to raise the subject in parliament.

As I stand talking here I do not at all have that easy feeling which a man ought to have when he is freely stating his opinions. The feeling I have is on the contrary that I am making use, in a pretty cowardly fashion, of a truce declared between the public and the men in power, or that I am taking advantage of a close season for writers and artists: how long it will last I don't know—perhaps till the winter, perhaps only till tomorrow. Just as I cannot believe that power and the citizen can ever see themselves as one, that the rulers and the ruled will ever go to singing lessons together, so I do not believe that art and power will ever cosily enjoy each other's company. They won't; they can't, ever. For they are different things and they don't suit one another. What *is* possible and lends some prospect to our efforts is this: that these two, power and the citizen, will understand one another's position and work out a decent set of rules for getting along together. Even writers are human; and ruling circles are made up of human beings too. If one of us by a quirk of chance were to find himself belonging to some agency of political power, it would induce its own polarity in him and he would start having trouble with himself. Take a freedom-loving man, endued with a little egotism of course and concerned with his own cleanliness a little more than with the dirt around him, just by a decisive margin of a millimetre—a man who sees the complexity of things but madly wishes they were simple—a poet, say, or a musician: he'll not join the apparatus of state power. A poet in the cabinet—that's only a graceful little nod in the direction of power. I am speaking here of the incompatibility of two things, not of enmity necessarily. I will tell you of an experience I had that has come back to my mind several times these last two days. In April of last year I was present, as one of the editors of *Literární noviny*, at a meeting in the Ideological Department of the Party's Central Committee. The outcome of the meeting was not, for us, a success. I was seated at a table exactly opposite one of the Central Committee Secretaries, Comrade Jiří Hendrych, so that instead of the usual impression of a mere outline I suddenly had a close-up sight of the face of a man older than myself—I was brought up to raise my hat to people that much older—the face of a man who was now transformed for me from an institution into somebody with worries like myself; personal, professional and perhaps other kinds of worries, certainly weightier than mine, and ones he had had to live with for a long time. I didn't speak very effectively on that occasion. I had intended to be completely candid and sincere, but I had been scared and defensive. I had an idea that they were reading other motives into my behaviour. When they began whispering to each other I succumbed to a feeling of helplessness; this humiliated me and I lost my temper. When I went home later, apart from other confused thoughts about the whole scene, one completely new idea forced itself on my mind, or rather a disturbing presentiment that quite upset the clear dichotomy of 'us' and 'them'. I felt a gust of wind from the unknown, an intimation of human suffering in a situation evidently ignored in the attitudes implied by phrases like 'class viewpoint' and 'opposition' that are used so much in our society. These are wartime expressions. I had to adopt for the time being some firm attitude, of course, in order to carry on at all at that meeting. And so I told myself that the suffering I had mentioned was part and parcel of the situation. It was simply that he felt a desire to act like that, though he need not have, and similarly that I wanted to stay on the newspaper. But the whole episode gave me a new incentive to think about power as a human situation. . . . However, I will end this digression and pick up where I left off. Even writers are people, and ruling circles are made up of human beings too. Not even writers want anarchy, for they like to live in nice towns and have nice flats, and they want other people to have them too; they want industry to prosper, they want businesses to make a profit. And this would not be possible without some organising effort by the government.

Art cannot abstain from discussing government, for to govern means, directly or indirectly, to make continuous administrative decisions about people's lives, about their wellbeing and their disappointments, about the subjects of their thoughts and about things that cannot be decided and are nevertheless for ever being decided. So art cannot abandon the criticism of government, seeing that governments, whoever they consist of and however they behave, are the product of national culture.

Our own government, let us say, pleases the artistic community by congratulating it on the handsome Czechoslovak pavilion at the World Fair. The government certainly likes saying this; it has political point and it may even be meant sincerely. However, this does not mean that the artists have to be pleased with the particular government that they have. The World Fair pavilion, which enjoys the cultural equivalent of extraterritorial rights in a way, simply proves what these same artists could do at home if they were allowed to, if they carried the same weight on their home ground. So I must confess to having asked myself very often whether we are not serving a deceitful purpose by putting up such a charming Pavilion of Culture to represent the country. For we know that our best efforts are unwanted; everything we do is haphazard; deadlines are agreed but we don't even know the date. Every cultural achievement, in fact everything worth while that our people have done, including every good piece of manufacture, every good building and every good application of thought in our laboratories, studies or institutes—all this has been in spite of the behaviour of our governing circles for years past, rather than because of it. It was done in literal defiance of our rulers. But I don't want to be unjust. I am sure that every move for improvement within these ruling circles, every attempt at a better style of ruling, is dearly paid for; someone or other suffers for it; and if some visible success is scored, it is scored in the teeth of resistance. So where is the guidance and the leadership? All I can see is someone applying the brakes. It has never happened to me in the last ten years that I felt, when listening to some official disquisition, Now here is a wonderful idea that nobody had before! On the contrary, sometimes my glum reaction was simply, So what? We've all known this for ages! But most frequently of all I ask myself: How am I going to rescue my own idea this time? I can't convince them, for I never meet them, so how can I pull the wool over their eyes?

My eyes and my ears tell me that power only retreats when it sees and hears strong resistance ahead. Not argument—they will never convince the men in power: only failure, recurrent failure with every attempt to do things the old way. Such failures are hard on us all, hard on our purses and our nerves. I see a continual desire to go back to the bad old days, and a continual danger that this will happen. For what do they amount to, these reminders that we have got our Writers' Union, that we have got our Literary Fund and our publishing house and our newspaper? They amount to a threat to take them away again if we do not behave. If I could tell myself that these things were originally theirs, I could say what my sister always says: One day He gives, another day He takes. But are these men really lords of creation? What are they prepared to leave in other hands than their own? Nothing at all? Then there is no need for us to be here at all. Let them say this, if they mean it. Let it be publicly shown that a handful of people, when you come to count them, claim the right to make life-and-death decisions about everything, about what is to be done, what thoughts are to be thought and what feelings felt. It is this that tells you something about the status of culture in a country, and gives you a picture of its level of civilisation, not the much-honoured and much-publicised individual works.

During the past season we have often had occasion to hear that the ruling circles have conceded a certain degree of autonomy to culture within its own field. But culture must not be surprised, we are told, if it gets rapped over the knuckles for straying into the field of politics. We are accused of forgetting our own principle, that all work should be done by experts. True, politics should also be run by experts. But how can you be sure that you have got experts for the job? I doubt it myself, and I prefer to use a metaphor to explain the reasons for my doubt. A doctor is certainly an expert. He is better fitted to diagnose our diseases than we are, and he can give us expert treatment. But he cannot claim to know better than ourselves how we feel under his treatment. And only a grossly inexpert doctor would submit us to a dangerous operation without first obtaining our written consent.

We are told that art and culture are autonomous now. This is a slogan, a tactic for the moment. Today the rules say this, tomorrow that, and there is an impression of change. But no one needs to be a great expert to see that, even if there are two taps, it all comes from the same barrel.

Just as I feel none too safe in the present state of cultural policy, which the ruling authorities are obviously in a position to push to the breaking-point, as a citizen I feel not too secure either once I am outside these four walls, this playground of ours. True, nothing unpleasant is happening to me; nothing happened to me in the past. That sort of thing isn't done any more, of course. Should I be grateful? I feel no inclination to be. I am afraid. I can really see no effective guarantees. I can see improvement in the working of our courts, but the judges themselves—they can see no effective guarantees either. I can see improvement in the work of our state prosecutors. But do the state prosecutors possess any guarantees, do they feel secure? If you like, I could interview some of them for our paper. Do you imagine it would get printed? I shouldn't be afraid to interview the chief prosecutor himself about, say, the reasons why people innocently sentenced and later rehabilitated never, of course, recover their original rights. We could discuss why the National Committees refuse to return them their flats or houses. But that will never appear in print. Why has nobody had the decency to apologise to such people? Why do the victims of political persecution enjoy no financial alleviations, why do they have to haggle about money? Why can we not live where we choose? Why can a tailor not go off to Vienna for three years, or a painter to Paris for thirty, and return when he likes without being made out a criminal? There is one principle which our Parliament is evidently very familiar with: *nullum crimen sine lege*— no law broken, no crime. It applies it by creating as many criminals for the state as it wishes. (Applause.) Why should not people who have decided they do not like it here go to the devil if they wish? And those who are not interested in seeing the completion of the democratic measures we have embarked upon, why should they not go away too?

It is true that a number of new and improved laws have been

passed. It is true that others are on the way. An amendment is being prepared to the law on the remaining civic freedoms—freedom of association and assembly. A draft is being worked on in the Ministry of the Interior. An article on the subject was set up for printing in *Literární noviny* and then confiscated. I see no guarantees. What guarantees are there? I cannot say, and I am coming to a stop now. For I have reached my last point, my great doubt: whether, namely, the ruling circles themselves, the cabinet and its individual members, have any guarantee in the exercise of civic freedoms without which no creative work can be done—not even creative politics. Here I end my account of the natural laws of power and I can only refer to a formulation which has been used elsewhere—something about a mill which often grinds up those who set it turning.

A measure of the level of culture really attained by a country is the extent to which functions indispensable for the orderly running of the state are exercised in a civilised fashion. Improvement of cultural policy is therefore not so important as a cultured style of politics generally. In countries where politicians display culture in their politics, no writer, artists, scholar or engineer has to exhaust himself in wrestling for his professional rights, his guild rights, his sectional rights, his parliamentary factional rights, his Cultural Union rights; he does not have to argue about the 'specific character of his work' or to provoke the resentment of the rest of the public, workers, farmers and officials, who are entitled to the same benefits as himself but lack the means to squeeze their ideas through the sieve of censorship, to transmute their sorrows and their moral pathos and give them artistic shape in structure or colour, in epigram or poem or musical composition. It is not bad cultural policy, but uncultured politics which kindles the flames of freedom-fights and then feels upset that the subject is still discussed, not realising that true freedom only exists where there is no need to talk about it. It feels upset when people say what they have seen yet instead of changing the things they see it keeps on trying to change their eyes. And meanwhile time runs out for the only thing worth everybody's yearnings—the dream of government identified with the public, the dream of the citizen who almost rules himself. Can it be made true, this dream?

In our search for this dream, aspired to by our two nations from the very depths of their history, we have seen a number of partial successes. One was the creation of an independent Czechoslovakia thanks to progressive popular forces and progressive politicians—this is not set down in the draft Standpoint and I propose that we put it there. For this was the birth of a state which for all its imperfections introduced a high degree of democracy by the standards of regimes existing at that period of history, and fostered in the minds and hearts of its citizens no particular aversion to those ideals of socialism which were to become feasible in the second stage of its development. (Applause.) The continuous aspiration toward a social welfare state changed, after the war, into a socialist programme as such. The particular conditions under which that programme was approached, notably the quality of socialism in the country where it already existed and the level of knowledge of socialism then prevailing, meant that distortions occurred in our country during the process of implementing socialism, along with events that cannot be explained away by the local climate and were not in line with the character or history of the nation. Whenever anyone mentions this period or asks for some explanation of why we then lost so much moral and material strength, and why our economy began to stagnate, our ruling circles reply that it was all necessary. From the point of view of all of us here I do not think it was necessary at all. Perhaps it was necessary for the spiritual development of those agencies of power which more or less obliged every supporter of socialism to go through the process with them. It cannot be overlooked that in the past twenty years not a single basic human problem in our country has been solved, from primary needs like housing, schools and economic wellbeing to those more subtle requirements which the world's undemocratic systems cannot fulfil—the feeling of playing a full role in society, for example, or the subordination of political decisions to ethical criteria, the belief in the importance even of humble work, the need for trust between individuals, or elevating the educational standards of the entire public. I am afraid we have not even improved our standing on the world stage; I sense that the name of our Republic has lost its healthy ring. I can see that we have failed to give mankind any original thoughts or bright ideas. We have no suggestion, for example, on how to be a manufacturing country without drowning in the products of manufacture. All we have done so far is to follow dumbly in the wake of de-humanised, American-style civilisation, reproducing the mistakes of East and West alike. Our society has no agency equipped to find an economical short cut across the grime and racket of evolution toward a better way of life.

I do not mean to say that we have lived in vain or that nothing is worth while. It has all been worth while: but only, perhaps, as a warning. Mankind's stock of knowledge would have increased in any event; there was no need for the lesson to be taught at the expense of a country whose civilisation was aware of the danger. I propose that the Standpoint be amended to include an account of what Czechoslovak progressive circles were aware of, or at least sensed, during the 1930's.

Recently I have got to know a large number of remarkably fresh personalities. A few individuals and a few collectives too; work teams and common interest groups. It was surprising the degree of resistance they showed. They had withstood the influ-ence of power and were obeying the natural principles of superior persons: work hard, keep your promises, don't betray your principles and don't let others get you down! Over and above these fairly traditional virtues of superior people they had acquired another good quality, viz. a lack of proper deference between subordinate and superior, between those in humble and those in higher stations. Strangely enough this repulsive trait common to every idle slacker nowadays, though only recently added to the classical list of good qualities, did really seem among these people like a new feature—the mark of a man who does not need to abase himself for bread.

In conclusion I should like to put one thing plainly, perhaps superfluously, for it surely emerges from everything I have said. None of my critique of power in this country is intended to decry socialism; for I am not persuaded that things need have turned out here the way they did and hence I cannot identify this power-system with the concept of socialism as the system itself tries to. Nor is there any reason why the two things should meet the same fate. And if the men who exercise this power—just for the moment I shall break the spell that associates them with power and

appeal to them as individuals with private thoughts and feelings—
if they were to come here and ask us one question, Can the dream
be made true? then we should have to consider it a sign of goodwill, and at the same time of supreme public spirit, if each of us
answered: I do not know.   (Applause.)

Notes

1. *Pavel Kohout*, popular playwright and representative figure of those in his generation who travelled the road from enthusiastic orthodoxy in their youth in 1948 to equally engaged revisionism twenty years later. He wrote the 'Petition of the Citizens' which appeared in a special issues of *Literární listy* on the eve of the meeting with the Soviet Politburo at Čierná nad Tisou on July 31, 1968, and was signed by many thousands of Czechs at booths set up in the streets of Prague and other cities.

2. *Literární noviny*, the magazine of the Czechoslovak Writers' Union, was descended from Prague's admirable pre-war liberal daily *Lidové noviny*, to which Karel Čapek was a notable contributor. It was changed into a weekly during the period of enthusiastic 'Sovietisation' that followed the communist take-over in 1948: the chief organ of the Soviet Writers' Union, after all, was a weekly. . . . After its rebirth as *Literární listy* in January 1968 it became the chief forum for the ideology of reform. Like most of the Czech press it went underground at the time of the invasion to emerge as *Listy*, fighting a stout rear-guard action against the reimposition of censorship and other restrictions of the counter-reformation until Husák suppressed it finally in April, 1969.

Kultúrny život, its Slovak counterpart, made its most important contribution at an earlier stage of the reform movement in 1963, preparing the way for Dubček's appointment as first secretary of the Slovak Communist Party.

3. *Václav Havel* is Czechoslovakia's most original and gifted dramatist, and a generation younger than most of the writers prominently associated with the reform movement. Born in 1936, the son of a millionaire who owned a rich slice of the commercial centre of Prague, he

was excluded from higher education and allowed to study at the Academy of Dramatic Art only a few years ago *after* he had become a successful creator of plays. Two of his essays in a rather special Czech version of the 'absurd' style—*The Garden Party* and *The Memorandum*— have been published (Cape Editions) and produced in England and many other countries. His passport was confiscated by the Czech government in the summer of 1969.

4. *Ludvík Vaculík*'s novel *Sekyra* (*The Axe*), published in Prague in 1966, is an original and deeply-felt statement of the experience of his generation (*b.* 1926) of Czech communists. His speech to the Congress (see Appendix) and his '2000 Words' manifesto will survive as the purest expressions of the particular style of socialist humanism that inspired the 'Prague spring' of 1968.

5. *Jiří Hendrych,* Novotný's chief ideological trouble-shooter, finally turned against his master in December 1967. He lost his place on the Party Presidium in the following March, and has not been restored to a position of influence by Husák.

6. *Eduard Goldstücker,* chairman of the Writers' Union in 1968, Professor of German at Charles University, Prague, ambassador to Israel, victim of the Slánský purges, and Kafka scholar, largely responsible for the rehabilitation of Kafka at a conference held in Prague in 1963. A Jew, and a popular, moderate exponent of Dubček's 'Socialism with a human face', he has been one of the most sharply attacked of all the reformers. Since 1968 he has been Visiting Professor of Comparative Literature at the University of Sussex.

7. *cadre register*: the nomenklatura system common to all countries in the Soviet bloc, whereby politically sensitive posts in every reach of society are controlled by the Party centre.

8. *A. J. Liehm,* foreign editor of *Literární listy,* a very clever political journalist and film critic, one of the chief sponsors of the Czech film revival. His valuable collection of long interviews with leading Czech writers was published in Vienna in 1968 (*Gespräch an der Moldau*: Molden Verlag), and in Paris in the following year with a scathing preface by Sartre.

9. *Ivan Klíma*, popular playwright, short-story writer and former member of editorial staff of *Literární noviny, Literární listy* and *Listy.*

10. *Alexander Kliment,* another *LN* journalist and novelist. His powerful fable about the techniques of power in a post-Stalin society, 'A Fear of Snakes', can be read in *New Writing in Czechoslovakia* (Penguin, 1969).

10a. *fraction,* here and elsewhere, denotes those members of any organisation who are also Communist Party members. As such they have to concert their attitudes and tactics and implement the line dictated to them by the appropriate Party body.

11. *Miroslav Holub,* a brilliant medical scientist as well as one of the most popular Czech poets. There is a good selection of his poems, well ıslated, in the Penguin Modern European Poets series.

12. *Jan Procházka,* novelist and vice-chairman of the Writers' Union in 1968, an early target of Soviet criticism. *Arnošt Lustig* is Czechoslovakia's most accomplished Jewish novelist, a survivor of Terezín and other Nazi concentration camps. Two of his novels—*Night and Hope* (1962) and *Dita Sax* (1966)—have been published by Hutchinson in England.

13. *Milan Kundera,* a Moravian like Vaculík, but a more sophisticated ironist, much influenced by Sartre. His novel *Žert* (It was published as *The Joke* by Macdonald in 1969 in an edition which took scandalous liberties with the original text, cutting some parts and rearranging the order of others. Kundera wrote a furious letter of protest to the TLS; and in 1970 Penguin produced a correct version with the cuts restored.) had something of the same impact as Vaculík's *The Axe* when it was finally allowed to appear early in 1967.

14. *Laco Novomeský,* veteran Slovak poet and communist, organiser of the Slovak Uprising of 1944 and close friend of Gustáv Husák, with whom he was imprisoned in 1954 as a 'Slovak bourgeois nationalist'. A fairly conservative communist, like Husák himself he found the pace of the reform movement of 1968 too rapid and its temper too radical. He resigned from the editorial board of *Kultúrny život* as a mark of his disapproval, and almost alone among writers of real stature in Czechoslovakia he lent his name to Husák's policies in 1969.

15. *Jiří Hájek,* not to be confused with the former Foreign Minister, was a literary critic, something of a 'licensed liberal' in the fifties, and a former editor of the Writer's Union monthly *Plamen.* An isolated figure in 1968, after his performance at the Congress, he has come into his own again as a noisy apologist for the counter-reformation, editing a new weekly, *Tvorba,* which rose as *Listy* went down.

16. *Miroslav Válek,* Slovak editor and poet of a rather old-fashioned surrealist kind. Left *Kultúrny život* with Novomeský early in 1968; chairman of the Slovak Writers' Union and Slovak Minister of Culture since 1969.

17. *Pavel Aueršperg,* Novotný's chief speech-writer until 1965, occupied the hot seat of head of the Party's ideological section until March 1967, when he was sacked for allowing liberalisation to go too far. His tenure saw the publication of Radovan Richta's massive report on the social implications of the scientific revolution, *Civilisation at the Crossroads,* and the launching of Zdeněk Mlynář's research into the political adjustments that the economic reforms might require. Aueršperg's fall left him very much disenchanted with the cause of reform, and he

was accused of acting as guide, philosopher and friend at the Soviet Embassy in Prague during its dire political difficulties in the first weeks after the invasion. In 1969 he became head of the international section of the Party Secretariat.

18. *Ladislav Mňačko,* Moravian-born Slovak novelist and top-flight journalist of the romantic, Hemingway-myth kind—two-fisted, hard-drinking, no respecter of persons. His *Belated Reports* published in Bratislava in 1964 was a fictionalised account of typical stories of official corruption and deception of the kind that no Czech or Slovak journalist could have dreamed of publishing at the time they occurred, in the early 'fifties. His critique of stalinism on Czechoslovakia was developed even more sensationally in the novel *A Taste for Power* (Weidenfeld & Nicolson, 1967) in which Novotný, to his rage, detected the outline of his own unpleasing character in the crude and narrow *apparatchik* Galovitch. Shortly after the invasion, Mňačko left to settle in Germany. *The Seventh Night* (Dent, 1968) is a rough and ready account of the first week of the invasion as it was seen in Bratislava, interspersed with 'confessional' recollections of his experience of his country's history since Munich.

19. *Miroslav Mamula,* the feared and detested party head of military intelligence, was strongly suspected of preparing the abortive military coup which Novotný hoped for in the last desperate days of his reign. He was the first senior *apparatchik* to be dismissed by Dubček and one of the last to be rehabilitated under Husák. In October 1969 it was announced that Party discipline against him had been stopped. His discharge had been 'unavoidable' owing to the 'incorrect methods' he had applied in the Novotný era, but he was to be 'speedily provided with employment in keeping with his political and specialised qualifications'.

20. *Jan Zelenka,* one of several Novotnýite hacks who got high preferment after April, 1969, is now director-general of Czechoslovak Television.

21. *The Majales procession,* an annual event for the students of Prague which got more and more eventful as the 'sixties wore on. On May 1, 1966, the procession was especially lively, shouting demands for freedom and democracy and ruderies at the security men. Twelve youngsters received prison sentences for their part in it.

Index

About the Author

DUŠAN HAMŠÍK, a highly respected Czech journalist, served as editor-in-chief of *Literární noviny* (in 1968 during the Prague Spring this newspaper was to win international fame as *Literární listy*) during the period described in this book. He is the author of several books published in Czechoslovakia, among them *A Bomb for Heydrich*, which was translated into several languages. He is currently at work on a biographical study of Himmler.